DATE DUE

Feb 28 '66	Mar 8 '77		
Apr 27 '66	Mar 20 78		
Mar 7 '69	20 78		
May 15 '72			
Oct 23 '72			
Dec 1 '72			
Sep 20 '73			
Oct 19			
Apr 24 '74			
May 8 '74			
May 31 '74			
Ma 3 '75			
Mar 7 '75			
Apr 7 '75			
Sep 24 '75			
Jan 26 '76			
Feb 9 '76			
Nov 9 77			

MODERN DANCE

for

High School and College

MODERN DANCE

for

High School and College

MARGERY J. TURNER, Ed.D.

New York University

Photographs by Bill Spilka

Englewood Cliffs, N.J.

PRENTICE-HALL, INC.

793.33
T85m

LIBRARY OF CONGRESS
CATALOG CARD No.: 57-9308

44337
Jan. 1963

First Printing ....*March, 1957*
Second Printing ....*May, 1960*

PRINTED IN THE UNITED STATES OF AMERICA

59097—C

To Two Great Teachers

THEODORA BURCH and THELMA HRUZA

Preface

THIS book grew out of a teaching situation in which students were required to take modern dance. Most of the students were disposed to dislike any activity—particularly one which required them to think for themselves and express their own ideas in movement. Clearly, then, the situation called for salesmanship; special efforts were needed in order to capture the interest of such a group. The surest, if not the only, road to this accomplishment lay through carefully planning and selecting materials that would reflect the needs and interest of the classes. To determine the effectiveness of the materials thus chosen, results were evaluated after each lesson; successful ideas were retained and unsuccessful ones reworked. Teaching dance became more and more interesting with each new experience. Soon the relationship of one lesson to another began to point so clearly to the larger, more important objectives that it was necessary to organize these ideas and put them on paper. This book is the culmination of those efforts.

If this book contained all the lessons successfully developed in the course of the experiences outlined above, however, it would be unwieldly; moreover, one might mistakenly conclude that it is intended to be a sort of formulary substitute for individual planning. Consequently, the lesson material has been condensed in order merely to show, by example, an approach to creative teaching. And the approach is actually quite simple. If the teacher follows it over a period of time and puts herself and her teaching methods to analytic test, she will discover many ways of providing creative experiences for others as well as for herself.

Because the book is built upon practical study and teaching experience, there is no bibliography. The content derives from assimilated study with many of the finest dance educators and professional dancers of our time. Their contribution to the field of dance has been great, and their influence on the author's thinking and teaching is unquestionable. The author takes pleasure in listing those people with whom she has studied:

> *Educational*—Theodora Burch, Shirley Genther, Alma Hawkins, Margaret H'Doubler, Louise Kloepper, Katherine Manning, Marjorie Parkin, Elizabeth Waterman, Theodora Wiesner.
>
> *Professional*—Hanya Holm, Doris Humphrey, Sophie Maslow, Alwin Nikolais, Sybil Shearer, Elizabeth Waters, Charles Weidman.

In addition to those listed above, the author is indebted to Anne Breaky for her constant co-operation and help throughout the original writing of this book; to Roscoe Brown for his assistance on the analysis of exercise; and to Jean Foss for further practical testing of materials and other time-consuming assistance.

MARGERY J. TURNER

Contents

1

Teaching
Modern
Dance

MODERN, or contemporary, dance is an art form that uses movement as a medium of expression. It is the result of intentional ordering of movement by a choreographer. The movement is created in response to the re-experiencing of emotional values, which are thus given a new existence. The expressive movement is highly selected, spatially designed, and organized through rhythmic structure; the result is the communication of an idea, mood, feeling state, or situation.

The student should come to know dance through her experiences with it—through experiences that are an essential and dynamic part of her life. This may be most effectively achieved through intelligent stimulation to creative activity and continued guidance during the developmental process. The teacher must provide the student with knowledge of how to work to achieve such success.

Dance is for all students to experience, within the limits of their capacities. The average student has more capacity than she thinks she has, and is very often surprised by what she can accomplish through this medium of expression. She should be encouraged to continue her development, even with limited capacity, for there are many other values which are by-products of dance experience. Whether or not a student becomes skilled in performance is of little importance educationally.

Most of the educational value in dance is achieved through problem solving. Therefore, the teacher's responsibility is to provide stimulating and interesting situations that call for problem solving activity. Through problem solving the student learns how to get at the root of a difficulty; how to meet barriers and conquer them; how to think logically, so that her idea will be communicated clearly; how to work with other people and share ideas; and how to evaluate creative projects that will benefit others as well as herself. All of these values will aid the student in understanding herself and others.

Through dance experience the student also develops a type of sensitivity that is basic to technique—kinesthetic awareness. Kinesthetic awareness is sensitivity to fine degrees of differentiation in movement and muscle action; it is also sensitivity to the responses of other people and situations, whether they exist in dance or in everyday living.

Dance is of particular importance in education because it lends itself readily to creative activity. However, it is not possible to "give" a student creative experience; the teacher can do no more than set the situation that stimulates such activity and guide it in its development. The actual creative act can be produced only by the student herself.

But though this discussion stresses the teacher's use of a creative approach, planned movement must also play an important role in modern dance training. In fact, preconceived movement is not only important: from the standpoint of developing co-ordination, it is essential. If one never taught set movement sequences, the student's movement education would be very narrow and incomplete. However, when movement sequences are taught, they should be taught for the purpose of broadening the student's perspective, so that she realizes how much more room she has for improvement. These sequences should be challenging in co-ordination, dynamics and rhythm, and they should be interesting and enjoyable to do. Locomotor movements are particularly valuable for release activities after a class has been working hard on a creative problem. By the same token, copying movement is of value if it is not overdone. It is a means of disciplining one's body by directing it to reproduce movement which was created by another person. Everyone has her own particular style of moving. By copying movement of others, the student experiences a style of movement different from her own, and this is an important part of broadening her learning experience. It is also a challenge to the student to reproduce movement of others that is accurate in form, rhythm, and quality.

Fundamental principles of movement and rhythmic accuracy should be stressed throughout the dance experience. It is not possible to isolate one facet of the total dance picture without losing its relationship to the whole. One can emphasize any one facet of the total dance experience only in relation to the overall picture.

For example, the teacher may design a composition problem based essentially on focus. But because she cannot isolate focus from direction, rhythm, space, and motivation without losing its value both as a relative principle and as a meaningful experience, she must merely emphasize it as the strong point of a whole composition. Such problems should be means to ends rather than ends in themselves, and the instructor should be sure that the student sees the relationship of means to end.

Dance in education is very much in need of higher standards of work. It has passed the stage of being considered just another recreational activity at which one plays for a season. If dance is to function in the lives of people, it must become a dynamic part of their experience, and this experience must be carried over a longer period of time. It is impossible to develop a broad understanding of dance in a short time. It is an accepted fact that every student does not desire to dance and that some students will be satisfied by just an acquaintance with it. This acquaintance should at least open their viewpoints to such an extent that they are able to understand dance as spectators and, with each new experience, grow in their understanding. Since the majority of students get a relatively short exposure to dance through classes, it is very important to have high standards of performance both in the professional groups that may be brought to the school and in the student performing group. The student performing group should function as an educational vehicle for the school at large. However, in their role they should not be exploited to the point of sacrificing their academic standing.

CREATIVE TEACHING

Creative teaching is a process that is conditioned by many factors. First among these factors are the viewpoints, attitudes, and philosophy of the teacher. It is the teacher who sets the climate for creative activity. A climate that perpetuates creative activity is one that is free and relaxed but well organized. It is free and relaxed in the sense that the student is in control of herself and does not feel inhibited from saying what she thinks or expressing what she feels is important. The atmosphere should be one conducive to learning and sharing ideas that will help to solve the problems of the group.

The creative teacher recognizes the futility of talking about educational values to someone who has no concept of them. She realizes that her only practical approach is through cultivation of her students' interests by providing situations and experiences through which they themselves will discover and appreciate personal values in education. If the subject has been introduced in this manner, the student will be able to identify educational principles with her own experiences. Thus, the discussion becomes a verification of ideas the student herself has developed; and these ideas, in turn, play a more dynamic part in her conscious experience.

The creative teacher stimulates the creative powers of the student. When the creative urge is active, the student's behavior becomes highly inventive and searching, and curiosity is ever present. The principles she discovers during the creative process become the foundation from which further creative growth may spring. Every adult realizes as a result of her own experiences that there is nothing quite so convincing as something one discovers for oneself.[°]

The creative teacher inspires a drive for problem solving in her students which results in a particular kind of working attitude. This attitude is displayed in attacking a problem with concentrated effort at the time it is presented. Students often function on a basis of procrastination and lethargy. Students who display this attitude are generally uninterested and consider their activities unimportant. It is the teacher's responsibility to make what she is teaching vital, dynamic, and interesting. Again, she must capture the interests of the students, not through verbal enthusiasm, but through ingenuity in approach. At the same time, she answers the needs of the group she is teaching. The teacher must live what she believes and believe that what she is teaching has an important contribution to make to the education of the student.

The creative teacher possesses spontaneity and ingenuity. She is sensitive to reactions of individuals and the effect these reactions have on the group. She is highly critical and keen in her observations of people. These personality characteristics are necessary if the teacher is to be equipped with the means for making the right decision at the right time. In classes there are many instances where the teacher may make or break a situation; this situation, in turn, may have far-reaching effects on student accomplishment and formation of attitudes.

The creative teacher is broad in her viewpoints and ingenious in her method of handling people. Her approach is one which stimulates the student to respond in such a manner that the resultant experience in dealing with the subject will provide the student with broader viewpoints. The outcome of such experience is one of discovery of principles related to living. Many of these experiences are intangible and exist emotionally and kinesthetically and do not lend themselves to verbal description. On the other hand, many of these experiences are tangible; for instance: the inhibited student who learns to lift her chest and experience a new sense of self-assertion in carriage as part of her daily life has discovered and applied a principle related to living; and an individual who, in a group creative project, learns the importance of considering the suggestions of others for a more efficient functioning of the group has learned a principle that will make her road to personal adjustment a great deal easier.

Creative teaching, then, does not consist simply in being able to get students to create their own dances; one can do that without teaching creatively at all. Rather, creative teaching is a continuous process of stimulation and guidance through which the student develops physically, emotionally, and intellectually and actively applies her knowledge to other phases of living.

Students who are exposed to creative teaching are more experimental in their approach to learning. They are more actively interested in solving problems through their own effort. They are more critical in their attitudes and do not gullibly accept information as fact without question. They think for themselves and try to relate new ideas and information to larger concepts and to other areas of study and living. Their questions show a thought process working within a broad frame of reference; they do not pigeon-hole ideas, as do all too many of our students and adults today. They become actively interested in their living processes. They feel a need for education in order to satisfy their intellectual curiosity.

Creative teaching is a continuous process which provides both the route and guideposts for continued individual development. It is an approach to teaching which allows for broad student experience through problem solving. This process of discovery, realization, and application should start in the beginning dance experiences and continue to grow, for there is no end. When the student leaves school she should have an approach to learning that will enable her to continue growing whether or not she attends another educational institution. The creative experience in the early stages of development may be as simple as discovering a sense of suspension through the chest as a result of proper co-ordination and timing, and it is a continuum of growth to the other extreme, at which the individual has developed her creative powers to the degree that her experience and understanding of the subject provide her with the necessary means for creating, in artistic form, any idea she wishes to express.

QUALIFICATIONS OF THE CREATIVE TEACHER

The creative teacher has a firm belief in the value of the subject she is teaching. Her own creative experience is adequate to enable her to understand the problems the student meets through such experiences. The creative teacher is spontaneous and unregimented in her teaching but is well organized and concrete in conducting her classes. She strives to maintain high standards of artistic work in her students. She maintains a balanced viewpoint on what is possible and practical to expect from her students. She does not impose her ideas on students, but rather, she helps them develop their own ideas. She realizes that her role in education is to broaden individuals artistically and intellectually as well as to develop their understanding of the use of the body as a means of expression. She is well grounded in her field and posesses integrated knowledge of her subject in relation to other subjects and to people. She applies this knowledge in her teaching. She knows the laws that govern movement, and she has a thorough understanding of the structure and function of the body. She is adaptable in her methods of teaching when she has difficulties with her classes. She realizes that student response depends greatly on the degree and kind of stimulation she provides. She has a clear understanding of the needs of her group both from their viewpoint and her own. The creative teacher is in the teaching field because she is interested in people and in what she can contribute to them. She feels a responsibility toward educating her students for successful living and has faith in their ability to find their place as useful citizens in a democratic society.

THE CREATIVE PROCESS

The creative process is an exciting and rewarding educational experience for both the student and teacher. It is a dynamic and unlimited learning experience that involves the total person in many kinds of learning activity. It is a process of adventure, exploration, and discovery that opens up many avenues of learning. The creative process is a process of becoming completely involved in one's activities; interacting with ideas and people in a problem solving situation; seeing new relationships; feeling alive, active, and vital; broadening one's concepts in relation to the subject being studied; replacing old concepts with new ones; questioning one's own ideas, beliefs, and values; developing the imagination; finding new ways of communicating; experimenting and selecting; organizing ideas into meaningful and artistic form; discovering principles related to living; understanding people and developing more democratic attitudes; learning how to work with others; setting goals; solving problems one has a need for solving; enlarging one's perspective with the acquisition of knowledge and achievement; and evaluating one's own progress.

The creative process is a total and dynamic kind of learning in which the student takes the responsibility for piloting her own course of adventure, faces and solves the problems she meets, and arrives at new roads of understanding. It is a process of emerging or becoming.

The beginning stages of the creative process are concerned

with the objective phase of movement experience. This phase consists of experimentation with movement for the joy of moving and sensing movement that is rhythmically organized. The student becomes aware of various degrees of tensional relationships of body parts, the dynamics of movement produced by contrast, spatial relationships of movement, projection of movement, and physical efficiency in the execution of movement. As the student gains movement experience, she also associates ideas and feelings with movement. These associations are based on her own experiences. This leads her into the subjective phase of experiencing movement, which establishes an awareness of motor imagery. She selects a particular phase of her experience, consciously organizes it in movement form, and thus enters a phase of maturation that becomes a challenging and enlightening stage of her development.

Before the individual can effectively attempt dance-creation, she must have motor imagery on which she can construct her movement. Thus, the early stages of teaching should be concerned with developing such imagery. This development will not be brought about by a cut and dried association of ideas and movement, however; the teacher must do an imaginative job of drawing ideas from the students and making them aware of the fact that the organic form of movement has suggestive content and is appropriate for the expression of that content (see composition problem 4, p. 129).

There are many different approaches to the actual creation of a dance. The particular approach the teacher uses in the beginning should be based on the needs of the group. Most people feel more secure when they are given something concrete on which to construct movement. For example, after enacting a given specific situation in pantomine, the movement may be changed from its realistic form and made more abstract by various means (see composition problem 1, p. 122). Or, the instructor may start with gesture and experiment with variation of that gesture. But no matter what approach is used, in order to do accurate work in abstraction, one must be accurate in the acting out of the situation or the gesture as the case may be. Movement is abstracted for the purpose of making it more highly suggestive rather than definitive as are pantomime and gesture in their natural form. Movement in its abstract form leaves more room for individual interpretation and becomes a more flexible vehicle for communication. On the other hand, if a group is highly spontaneous and has had considerable experience in improvisation, they might easily start with moods, characterization, or pure dance. There is no one "best approach" for everyone, because so much depends on the background and experience of the group.

NATURE OF A CREATIVE LESSON

The nature of a creative lesson has distinct characteristics of climate, approach, and evaluation.

Climate: The creative lesson fosters a permissive climate which is conducive to individual expression without fear of embarrassment or feelings of inadequacy. It stimulates search and exploration of the unknown. It requires the student to relate herself to many situations. It stimulates the student to discover expressive movement ideas that are new to her. The climate of a creative lesson is one in which students respect the rights of others to think and feel as they wish and at the same time have regard for the integrity of others.

Approach: The creative lesson begins with simple movement that is the same for everyone. This is followed by individual exploration and variation of movement, which develops into problem solving activity. The teacher organizes the situation by spontaneously making use of the direction of development that is suggested through the activity of the students. She allows developments to take place naturally; she does not force movement into a preconceived organization. The approach stimulates the development of spontaneity and adaptability in the student as well as in the teacher. The approach is characterized by the concentration of attention on a principle or problem to be considered. This problem is carried through a gradual process of development in which each student experiments individually within the framework of the class organization. The responsibility of making decisions rests with the student. The approach lacks a bound system of rules; rather, the student individually diagnoses her problem and searches for an answer that reveals logical and functional principles she can accept.

Evaluation: Evaluation of a creative lesson is a means of qualitative measurement of goal-reaching. It is a process of objectively analyzing the outcomes of class experience and the creative process. The purpose of evaluation of creative effort is to develop the students' ability to critically analyze their projects in light of their progress in meeting the goals they have set for themselves. The evaluation process is also concerned with drawing the common experiences of a lesson into an integrated whole. This should be a shared experience among the students, with the teacher acting mainly as a co-ordinator in the group discussion. Critical analysis functions on an impersonal basis and is focused on what was done rather than on the individual inadequacies of the person who did it. There should be no arbitrary or teacher-imposed set of standards that are considered "best" for all students, if individual progress is what is sought for. The conclusion of a creative lesson simply brings the problem solving activity to a temporary rest, since each evaluation period brings to a conscious level new goals and problems to be solved.

2

Body

Conditioning

Body conditioning is an essential part of dance education. The immediate objective of body conditioning is to develop strength, flexibility, co-ordination, agility, and control. The development of these attributes is useful primarily as a stepping stone to the attainment of broader objectives.

These broader objectives, of which the specific objectives are an integral part, are by-products of good teaching. The broader objectives envision the development of a well-controlled body that will respond to the needs of the individual in her creative endeavors. The attainment of these higher goals is also evident when an individual displays intelligent discrimination between fine differences in movement quality, when she fulfills a movement phrase with rhythmic accuracy, and when she displays kinesthetic understanding of movement.

In order to achieve these objectives the student must be taught basic information about the structure and function of her body. She must be given goals to work toward, and she must be instructed in methods of achieving these goals. Students who exercise without knowledge of principles of movement efficiency generally compensate through poor movement habits. This practice often results in little or no value from the exercises. If a goal is clearly defined when an exercise is taught, students will have some means of testing their own progress. For example, consider for a moment the familiar "stretching exercises" in a sitting position with the legs spread apart. The value in most stretching exercises is probably in the kinesthetic awareness of the tension that is produced in the muscles being stretched. The range of the leg spread may become greater due to voluntary control of relaxation in the muscles being stretched and tension in the muscles producing the leg spread. The range may also be increased through general increased flexibility in the hips. It necessarily follows that passive stretching (stretching by leaning dead weight against a joint or by force of another person) is of little or no value unless muscular control is adequate to make use of the increased range. Such exercises are done most efficiently when the muscles that cause the legs to spread are actively working and effort is being exerted voluntarily to relax the muscles being stretched. Students should also learn that there is an optimum for range of movement. They should learn to recognize optimum range for a given exercise so that they do not work beyond it. Coordination, which is a part of all movement, should be taught in relation to both the structure of the body and the direction a movement takes spatially, so that students gradually become motorly oriented in space.

Students should also be told what an exercise is for and the part of the body it is designed to affect. One of the most common sources of confusion is the misunderstanding of the function of abdominal muscles when the hip flexors and abdominal muscles are involved in the same exercise. Efficient co-ordination of muscle groups can be learned through conditioning exercises if they are well taught. When one learns to co-ordinate specific muscle groups intelligently, movement sensitivity is developed, and there is evidence of by-products that extend into the dance realm directly.

The exercises that follow this discussion are organized according to the parts of the body they are designed to affect. Following each exercise is a statement of its specific value. Values, of course, are relative to the conditions under which the exercises are done. A positive statement that an exercise strengthens a certain muscle group is not necessarily true. If a student happens to have a great deal of strength already, the exercise will function as an exercise for that muscle group but will not necessarily develop strength. There are other factors affecting the development of strength. One must overload the muscle group in order to strengthen it. The factors of speed and force in exercise are also important in the development of strength. The time factor is important in exercise of flexibility, but here the time is lengthened rather than shortened. Consequently, the question of the number of times an exercise should be done is left to the judgment of the teacher. This judgment will vary with the level of skill in different classes. In the few exercises that prescribe a definite number of repetitions, the number refers to a minimum of repetitions necessary in order for the student to derive any value from the exercise, or the number is listed merely as a means of giving the unit organization of the exercise. Each exercise also offers many smaller values that have not been listed. Space does not permit a full kinesiological analysis of each exercise, nor would such analyses be consistent with the purpose of this book. Therefore, only the primary values, and in some cases secondary values, are listed.

The following exercises represent only a sample from among the hundreds that are done in modern dance classes across the country. These exercises were selected for their functional contribution in developing well-controlled bodies. Their use is strongly recommended, but they are not proposed as a system that is superior to all other systems or as one which guarantees perfect results. The exercises are designed for specific purposes. The selection included here presents a well-rounded variety for attacking all parts of the body; emphasis is on the generally weaker areas of women.

CONDITIONING EXERCISES

A. WARMUP EXERCISES: The following exercises involve the total body and serve to increase circulation and respiration.

1. *Body Swings*

   a. *Starting position:* Standing with feet slightly apart and arms extended overhead.

   b. *Exercise:*

     (1) Forward and backward swings: Let the knees bend and the body collapse into a crouched position; immediately let the momentum carry the arms through to a backward swing while the knees straighten and the body remains in a forward bend.

     (2) Swing the arms down and forward letting the knees bend; continue the forward swing as the knees straighten and the body gradually straightens upward from a crouched position.

     (3) Sideward swings: Shift the weight to the right leg; let the body collapse over the right leg, swing the body over to the left leg, and stretch upward, keeping the weight left.

     (4) Let the body collapse over left leg; swing the body across to the right and extend upward.

     (5) NOTE: A true swing exists naturally in $\frac{6}{8}$ time. Swinging movement has three distinct characteristics—collapse, momentum, and suspension.

2. *Leg Swings*

   a. *Starting position:* Standing on the left leg, with the right leg extended backward and arms extended sideward.

   b. *Exercise:*

     (1) Swing the right leg straight forward from the hip, keeping the knee straight ahead and brushing the floor with the foot as the leg passes through.

(2) Swing the right leg backward through the same path.

(3) Keep the body stretched upward, the standing leg straight, and avoid any compensatory body movements.

3. *Arm Swings with Chest lift:*
   a. *Starting position:* Standing, with feet apart and arms extended sideward.
   b. *Exercise:*
      (1) Swing the arms downward and across the body, and at the same time, round the body forward and bend the knees.
      (2) Lift the arms upward, extend the body upward, and straighten the knees.
      (3) Swing the arms down and backward, and at the same time, bend the body backward from the knees.
      (4) Lift the arms upward, extend the body upward to a straight position, and straighten the knees.
      (5) NOTE: In extending the body, conscious effort should be exerted to lift the sternum and separate the sternum from the diaphragm.

4. *Relaxed Bounces*
   a. *Starting position:* Standing, with feet together and body in a relaxed bend forward and arms hanging.
   b. *Exercise:*
      (1) Relax the muscles in the back of the legs and keep the knees straight.
      (2) Bounce from the hips and try to get the palms of the hands to the floor.
      (3) Bounce in a semi-circle close to the feet, progressing from center to left to center to right.
      (4) Repeat the same bounces with feet in a wide stride.

5. *Knee Bounces*
   a. *Starting position:* Standing, with feet in wide stride, legs rotated outward, and arms at sides.
   b. *Exercise:*
      (1) Bend the knees at a ninety degree angle, keeping them directly over the feet.
      (2) Bounce in this position. Avoid sitting into the hips.

6. *Collapse and Extend*
   a. *Starting position:* Standing, with feet six inches apart and arms extended upward.
   b. *Exercise:*
      (1) Collapse to a squat position with back rounded forward in one count.
      (2) Gradually uncurl the body to the starting position in seven counts.

7. *Knee Grasp Exchange*
   a. *Starting position:* Lying on the back.
   b. *Exercise:*
      (1) Bend the right knee to the chest, grasp it with both hands, lift the extended leg six inches off the floor, and bring the chin to the bent knee.
      (2) Bend the left knee to the above position and extend the right leg.
      (3) NOTE: The alternate bending and extending of the legs should be rapid. The position of the lifted head and forward chin should remain constant.

8. *Body Bends*
   a. *Starting position:* Standing, with feet apart in a good stride and arms extended sideward.
   b. *Exercise:*
      (1) Bend the body forward from the hips with a flat

back. Bounce eight times and return to starting position.

(2) Place the right hand on the hip, extend the left arm straight upward and bend laterally to the right. Bounce eight times and return to starting position.

(3) Repeat exercise number two to the left, placing the left hand on the hip, extending the right arm straight upward and bending laterally to the left.

(4) Place both hands on hips and bend backward from the knees, keeping the back straight and the chest lifted. Bounce eight times and return to starting position.

(5) Repeat exercises one through **four,** taking four bounces in each position, then two, then one; and repeat the single bounce sequence.

9. *Prances*

 a. *Starting position:* Standing on the left leg, with right leg raised forward and bent at a right angle. The toes of the bent leg point directly to the floor. Arms are at sides.

 b. *Exercise:*

(1) Press the right leg into the floor. The toes touch first, followed by the ball of the foot and the heel. The knee straightens as the weight is transferred.

(2) Lift the left leg to the starting position as the weight is transferred to the right.

(3) Start at a slow tempo, gradually increase the tempo, and return to the slow tempo.

10. *Slow Running*

 a. *Starting position:* Standing, with weight inclined forward and knees slightly bent.

 b. *Exercise:*

(1) Lean forward until it becomes necessary to move the legs to avoid falling.

(2) Run as smoothly as possible, grasping the floor securely on each step.

(3) Exaggerate the push with the back leg and reach for the floor with the ball of the foot of the forward leg.

(4) Change direction quickly without changing pace.

B. EXERCISE FOR THE TRUNK AND PELVIC GIRDLE

1. *Back Stretch and Leg Lowering*
   a. *Starting position:* Lying on back, with arms extended sideward and palms against the floor.
   b. *Exercise:*
      (1) Lift the legs over the head and place the feet on the floor behind the head.
      (2) Bend the knees and straighten them four times.
      (3) Straighten the knees, grasp the ankles, and press the back against the floor. Keep the legs close to the body.
      (4) Release the ankles and lower the legs to the starting position. The lower back should be pressed against the floor while lowering the legs.
   c. *Value:* Strengthens hip flexors and abdominal muscles; stretches hamstrings and extensors of the back.

2. *Leg Flexion and Extension*
   a. *Starting position:* Lying on back.
   b. *Exercise:*
      (1) Bend the right leg to the chest and grasp behind the knee with the hands. Stretch the left leg away as the bent leg is pulled toward the chest.
      (2) Extend the bent leg straight upward; flex the knee and ankle as the leg is pulled toward the head; straighten the knee and ankle toward the ceiling. Repeat the flexion and extension of the knee and ankle seven times. With each repetition bring the leg closer to the head.

(3) Grasp the right leg with the right hand on the inside of the thigh; lower the leg to the right side, keeping it as close to the head as possible.

(4) Bring the leg back to starting position and repeat the sequence with the other leg.

c. *Value:* Stretches the hamstrings; strengthens hip flexors and abductors of the legs.

3. *Abdominal Contractions*
   a. *Starting position:* Lying on back, with arms at sides.
   b. *Exercise:*

   (1) Contract the abdominal muscles, causing the back to be rounded and the shoulders to leave the floor. Let the head hang back.

   (2) Release the contraction slowly. Repeat three times.

   (3) Contract the abdominal muscles so that the left shoulder is pulled toward the right hip. Remain flat on the back; release.

   (4) Repeat the diagonal contraction bringing the right shoulder to the left hip and release. Repeat the diagonal contractions six times, alternating sides.

   c. *Value:* Strengthens the oblique and rectus abdominal muscles and requires conscious effort in controlling one of the most important muscle groups.

4. *Sit-ups*
   a. *Starting position:* Lying on the back, arms extended sideward and palms upward. A partner assists by pressing the ankles of the active person to the floor.
   b. *Exercise:*

   (1) Lift the body off the floor, keeping the back straight and the arms in the same relative position.

   (2) Lower the body to the floor by pressing down first

the lower back and then the upper back, neck, and head.

   c. *Value:* Strengthens hip flexors on lifting phase and the abdominal muscles on the lowering phase. Contrasts the action of the two muscle groups.

5. *Sideward Lifts*
   a. *Starting position:* Lying on the right side, with the right arm extended and the head resting on the right arm; the left arm rests on the left side. A partner assists the active student in maintaining balance by straddling her at the knees and supporting her partner's thighs.
   b. *Exercise:*
      (1) Lift the shoulders, head, and arms toward the ceiling, and reach with the left arm toward the assistant.
      (2) Slowly return to starting position.
      (3) Keep the body perfectly straight. Bending at the hips will cause the student to roll off balance.
   c. *Value:* Strengthens the gluteals, oblique abdominals, serratus, and tensor facae latae.

6. *Lengthening Contraction*
   a. *Starting position:* Lying on back.
   b. *Exercise:*
      (1) Round the back, bend the knees, and bring the chin to the knees simultaneously.
      (2) Slowly straighten the legs and at the same time lower the shoulders until the body is almost straight.
      (3) NOTE: The hips and lower back remain in contact with the floor. When the body reaches an extended position, the legs and the head are a few inches off the floor.
   c. *Value:* Strengthens the abdominal and hip flexor

muscles. The abdominals function to stabilize the pelvis.

7. *Reverse Push-up*
    a. *Starting position:* Lying in a prone position, with weight resting on forearms, which are placed directly below the shoulders. Toes are extended so that the top of the foot rests on the floor.
    b. *Exercise:*
        (1) Contract the abdominal muscles to raise the body from its arched position to a position which is straight from head to toes.
        (2) Lower the body to starting position.
    c. *Value:* Strengthens the abdominal muscles and, secondarily, the upper back muscles in stabilizing the shoulder girdle.

8. *Push-ups*
    a. *Starting position:* Lying in a prone position, with legs spread and rotated outward. The hands are placed below the shoulders with elbows bent and palms downward.
    b. *Exercise:*
        (1) Tighten the body, push with the arms, and straighten the elbows, thus raising the body from the floor while maintaining alignment.
        (2) Lower the body to the floor, maintaining alignment.
    c. *Value:* Strengthens muscles of the shoulder girdle, pectorals, triceps, and abdominals.

9. *Circle and Lift*
    a. *Starting position:* Sitting, with legs spread and body rotated to the left.
    b. *Exercise:*
        (1) Swing the body from the base of the spine in a circle parallel to the floor. Progress from a rotated

position left to center and around to a rotated position right, and place the right hand on the floor behind the body.

(2) Raise the hips off the floor, extend the left arm, and reach toward the ceiling.

(3) Lower the body to the floor, repeat the circular sweep to the left, and raise the hips while resting on the left arm.

(4) NOTE: The hips should be lifted as high as possible and both hips should be level.

c. *Value:* Increases flexibility of spinal rotators and lateral flexors of the trunk; strengthens the hip and back extensors.

10. *Sitting Bounces*
   a. *Starting position:* Sitting straight, with legs spread.
   b. *Exercise:*
      (1) Round the back over the left leg and grasp the leg at as low a point as possible.
      (2) Bounce in this position, getting the body progressively closer to the leg. Do not return to original position after each bounce.
      (3) Repeat the bounces rounded forward and grasping both legs; then, repeat the bounces over the right leg.
      (4) NOTE: The bounces should be small and concentrated in the hips.
   c. *Value:* Stretches the extensors of the hip and increases flexibility of the hip joints and adductors.

11. *Bounce and Stretch*
   a. *Starting position:* Sitting upright, with legs extended straight ahead.
   b. *Exercise:*
      (1) Round the body forward and grasp the ankles.
      (2) Bounce four times and remain forward.
      (3) Extend the back by pushing through at the base

of the spine and straightening successively each
part of the back from the base of the spine to the
head. The arms reach forward and over the head.

c. *Value:* Strengthens extensors of the back, stretches
leg and hip extensors and increases flexibility in the
hip joints.

12. *Hip Extension*
   a. *Starting position:* Sitting, with weight on the left side
   and the left leg bent in front of the body and the
   right leg bent in back of the body. The left foot is at
   the midline of the body.
   b. *Exercise:*
      (1) Extend the right hip, keeping legs in contact with
      the floor.
      (2) Release the hip and sit into the floor with weight
      centered. Repeat seven times.
      (3) Reverse the starting position and do the exercise
      with the left hip.
   c. *Value:* Localization of the muscle group that produces extension in the hip joint.

13. *Pelvic Shift*
   a. *Starting position:* Kneeling, with the body in a vertical position and insteps resting on the floor.
   b. *Exercise:*
      (1) Slowly lower the hips to the left side while stretch-
      ing the body and arms to the right side.
      (2) Contract the abdominal muscles, gluteals, and
      thighs, and lift the hips forward and off the floor.
      (3) Shift the hips from the left side to the right and
      lower the hips to the right side while stretching
      the body and arms to the left.
      (4) NOTE: The exercise can be continually repeated
      on one side by dropping the knees to the right
      after lowering the hips.

c. *Value:* Strengthens extensors of the hips, adductors of the leg, and abdominal muscles.

14. *Climbing*
   a. *Starting position:* Lying on the back, with right leg extended upward at a right angle to the body.
   b. *Exercise:*
      (1) Grasp the knee of the right leg and climb upward as far as possible.
      (2) Climb downward to starting position. Repeat three times.
      (3) Raise the left leg and repeat the exercise.
   c. *Value:* Strengthens the abdominal muscles and lateral flexors of spine; stretches the hamstrings of the raised leg.

15. *Trunk Twisting*
   a. *Starting position:* Sitting straight, with legs spread apart.
   b. *Exercise:*
      (1) Twist the trunk as far to the left as possible and place both hands on the floor behind the hips.
      (2) Twist the trunk as far to the right as possible and place the hand on the floor behind the hips. This exercise should be done at a moderately fast tempo.
   c. *Value:* Increases flexibility of spinal rotators; stretches hamstrings and lateral flexors of the spine.

C. Exercises for the Pelvis and Legs

1. *Leg Circles*
   a. *Starting position:* Lying on back, with the right leg extended upward at a right angle to the body. Arms are extended sideward with palms against the floor.
   b. *Exercise:*
      (1) Lower the leg across the body until it is a few

inches from the floor. Keep the lower back pressed into the floor.

(2) Rotate the leg outward and move it through a circle parallel to the floor until it is out to the right side.

(3) Lift the leg directly to the starting position.

(4) Reverse the direction and lower the leg to the right, swing it around to the left side, and lift to starting position.

(5) Alternate the directions and repeat with the left leg.

c. *Value:* Increases flexibility of the hip joint; strengthens the adductors and abductors of the leg; secondarily strengthens abdominals.

2. *Hip Lift*
   a. *Starting position:* Sitting straight, with legs spread apart and hands on the floor behind the body.
   b. *Exercise:*
      (1) Lean back and raise the hips until the body is in a straight line. Keep the legs straight and maintain the spread position.
      (2) Lower the hips to the floor and assume starting position. Repeat seven times.
   c. *Value:* Strengthens hip and leg extensors.

3. *Leg Extensions Sitting*
   a. *Starting position:* Sitting to the left side, with left leg bent in front and right leg bent in back. Both legs rest on the floor with the left foot at the midline of the body.
   b. *Exercise:*
      (1) Shift the weight over the forward leg and keep the body upright.
      (2) Lift the right leg, extend it directly sideward and a few inches from the floor.
      (3) Bend the right leg and bring back of the body.

(4) Extend the right leg directly backward and bring it back to the starting position.

(5) Shift the weight over the right leg and keep the body upright.

(6) Lift the left leg and extend it upward and diagonally forward. Bend the left knee, bringing the foot back to the body without touching the floor, and repeat the extension of the left leg again.

(7) Reverse the position and do the complete exercise sitting to the right side.

c. *Value:* Strengthens the adductors and extensors of the hip and leg. Strengthens flexors of hip, extensors of knee, and abductors of the leg on the forward lift.

4. *Balancing*

a. *Starting position:* Standing, with heels together, legs turned out at a right angle, and weight centered over both feet.

b. *Exercise:*

(1) Shift the weight over the right leg and lift the left leg off the floor.

(2) Shift the weight as far as possible into the right hip.

(3) Change from one body position to another and experiment with compensations necessary to maintain balance.

(4) Go back to starting position and contrast the difference between passive hanging against the hip joints and active gripping in the hip to control balance.

(5) NOTE: The shift of the hips is sideward and parallel to the floor. The hips must be centered over one leg instead of two.

c. *Value:* Combines kinesthetic experience of controlling balance over a small base with understanding of mechanical factors of balance.

5. *Leg Swings with Hold*
   a. *Starting position:* Standing, with heels together, legs rotated out at a right angle, and arms extended sideward.
   b. *Exercise:*
      (1) Shift the weight over the left leg, stabilize balance, and stretch the body upward.
      (2) Swing the right leg forward, backward, forward, and hold it in the forward extended position for one count.
      (4) Repeat the sequence three times, shift weight to the right leg, and do the whole exercise with the left leg.
      (5) Shift the weight to the left leg again, with the right leg extended sideward on the floor.
      (6) Swing the right leg across the body with the knee bent and leg rotated outward; swing the same leg out to the side and extend it; repeat the swing across the body and hold for one count.
      (7) Swing the right leg out to the side in an extended position, across the body, out to the side again, and hold for one count.
      (8) Repeat from six with the left leg. The swinging leg is rotated outward throughout the exercise.
   c. *Value:* Strengthens hip flexors, extensors of the hip and knee, and outward rotators of the leg.

6. *Plié* (see analysis in Chapter 3, page 73).

7. *Leg Lifts*
   a. *Starting position:* Standing on the left leg, with the right leg extended backward and both legs rotated outward at a ninety degree angle. The arms are extended sideward.
   b. *Exercise:*
      (1) Lift the right leg forward from the hip, keeping both knees straight and the body upright.

(2) Actively pull the leg back to starting position. Repeat three times.

(3) Rotate the right leg outward and lift it directly sideward.

(4) Actively pull the leg to starting position. Repeat three times, alternating the return position between placing the foot in front and in back of the standing leg.

(5) Lift the right leg backward in an outward rotated position.

(6) Actively pull the leg back to starting position and repeat three times.

(7) Shift the weight to the right leg and do the whole sequence on the other leg.

c. *Value:* Strengthens the extensors and outward rotators of the leg and extensors and flexors of the hips.

8. *Leg Extensions*

a. *Starting position:* Standing on the left leg, with the right knee raised and the hands clasped under the thigh.

b. *Exercise:*

(1) Pull the bent leg up close to the body and stretch the standing leg.

(2) Extend the right leg forward, assisting the lift only as much as is needed.

(3) Bend the knee and bring the leg close to the body. Repeat three times.

(4) Bring the leg out to the right side in a bent position and grasp the inside of the thigh with the right hand.

(5) Extend the leg sideward and bend it again. Repeat three times.

(6) Lift the bent leg over the hip into a lifted position in back of the body; grasp under the thigh with the right hand.

(7) Extend the leg backward and bend it toward the body again. Repeat three times.

(8) Shift the weight to the right leg and repeat the whole exercise with the left leg.

c. *Value:* Strengthens flexors of the hips on forward and sideward extensions; strengthens extensors of hips and legs on backward lifts; strengthens outward rotators of the leg on the sideward lift; strengthens adductors of the standing leg.

9. *Leg Beating*

a. *Starting position:* Lying in a prone position, with arms folded and head resting on hands.

b. *Exercise:*

(1) Extend the right leg as far as possible.

(2) Lift the right leg as high as possible, keeping the hips on the floor.

(3) Take a series of thirty small and fast beats upward from the highest point of the lift, keeping the leg extended throughout the exercise.

(4) Repeat with the left leg.

c. *Value:* Strengthens the extensors of the hips and legs, and abdominals.

10. *Deep Knee Bends*

a. *Starting position:* Standing in a wide stride position.

b. *Exercise:*

(1) Bend the knees as far as possible, keeping the heels on the floor and the body straight.

(2) Shift the weight over the left knee and take a deeper bend, letting the heel rise.

(3) Raise the body as it is shifted through the center and over the right knee. Take a deep knee bend on the right leg.

(4) Repeat the rise, shift, and bend three times.

c. *Value:* Strengthens the extensors of the legs and hips.

D. EXERCISES FOR THE UPPER BACK AND SHOULDER GIRDLE

1. *Successive Uncurling*
   a. *Starting position:* Kneeling, with the hips resting on the heels, insteps flat on the floor, the head resting on the knees, and arms at the sides of the body.
   b. *Exercise:*
      (1) Gradually straighten the back to an upright position by uncurling the spine. Start the straightening at the base of the spine and carry the movement successively up the spinal column.
      (2) Extend the lower back as the head reaches the upright position. Continue the extension into the upper back and neck, and bend the body forward from the hips in this position until the body is parallel to the floor.
      (3) Round the body, drop the head forward, and begin again.
   c. *Value:* Increases flexibility of the back and provides practice in alternate relaxation and tension of opposing muscle groups of the trunk.

2. *Back Lift*
   a. *Starting position:* Standing, with feet together, body rounded forward, knees straight, and hands grasping the back of the ankles.
   b. *Exercise:*
      (1) Bring the body as close to the legs as possible with six small bounces.
      (2) Push through from the base of the spine, reach forward with the body and arms, and extend the back until it is parallel to the floor.
   c. *Value:* Strengthens extensors of the back and hips.

3. *Upper Back Extension*
   a. *Starting position:* Lying in a prone position, with arms extended diagonally forward. A partner assists

by pressing the active student's ankles against the
floor.

b. *Exercise:*
   (1) Lift the trunk, arms, and head toward the ceiling
      simultaneously.
   (2) Return to starting position.
   (3) NOTE: The abdominal muscles should be active
      to counteract the hyperextension in the lower
      back. The shoulders should be down and the
      neck stretched.
c. *Value:* Strengthens the extensors of the back and
shoulder girdle, and the levators of the arms.

4. *Shoulder Stand*
  a. *Starting position:* Lying on the back, with arms at
    sides and palms against the floor.
  b. *Exercise:*
    (1) Lift the legs over the head as in a backward roll.
    (2) Raise the legs slowly upward until a straight
       shoulder stand is reached.
    (3) Spread the legs apart, first sideward and then for-
       ward and backward. Maintain a straight extended
       position throughout the exercise.
    (4) Lower the legs behind the head and repeat.
  c. *Value:* Strengthens the extensors of the back and
    abdominals.

5. *Sitting Extension*
  a. *Starting position:* Sitting, with feet flat on floor, knees
    bent, back rounded, head on knees, and hands grasp-
    ing knees.
  b. *Exercise:*
    (1) Extend the back by starting the movement at the
       base of the spine and carrying it successively up
       the back.
    (2) Extend arms sideward and maintain the extended

position for eight counts. Return to starting position.

(3) NOTE: The shoulders should be down and the feet as close to the body as possible.

c. *Value:* Strengthens the extensors of the upper back and neck, and the levators of the arms.

6. *Side Lying Contraction-Extension*
   a. *Starting position:* Lying on the right side, with weight on right forearm.
   b. *Exercise:*
      (1) Round the body forward, bring the left knee to the chest, and swing the left arm backward.
      (2) Extend the body, lifting the leg in back and swinging the left arm in a circle forward and overhead to a full extension.
      (3) NOTE: In both the contraction and extension, the center of the body is the focal point. The movement of the extremities is toward that center and away from it.
   c. *Value:* Increases flexibility of total back extension.

7. *Twisting Swing*
   a. *Starting position:* Standing, with feet apart and arms extended sideward.
   b. *Exercise:*
      (1) Stabilize the hips and keep the feet stationary.
      (2) Twist the upper body to the right.
      (3) Alternate the twist from left to right, keeping arms in the same relative position to the body.
      (4) Maintain the exercise in a swinging rhythm.
   c. *Value:* Increases flexibility of trunk rotation.

8. *Trunk Swinging*
   a. *Starting position:* Standing with feet apart, body bent forward and parallel to the floor and arms extended sideward.

b. *Exercise:*
  (1) Swing the trunk, parallel to the floor, toward the right leg.
  (2) Swing the trunk around to the left leg.
c. *Value:* Increases flexibility of back extensors.

9. *Back Extension—Closed Position*
  a. *Starting position:* Sitting, with soles of feet together and hands grasping ankles.
  b. *Exercise:*
    (1) Round the back forward with head reaching toward floor.
    (2) Bounce eight times in this position.
    (3) Pull the knees down and straighten the back by pushing through the hips and extending the body forward.
    (4) Return to straight sitting position.
  c. *Value:* Strengthens back extensors and outward rotators of the legs; increases flexibility of hip joints.

10. *Back Extension—Open Position*
  a. *Starting position:* Sitting upright, with legs in wide spread.
  b. *Exercise:*
    (1) Round the back forward and grasp the ankles.
    (2) Bounce eight times in that position.
    (3) Push through the hips, reach forward with the arms, and extend the back; at the same time, increase the outward pull of the legs.
    (4) Circle the arms backward and make an additional effort to lift the chest on arrival at starting position.
    (5) Repeat steps three and four twice before beginning the exercise again. On each repetition of pushing forward from the hips, try to lift the hips off the floor.
  c. *Value:* Strengthens back extensors, shoulder girdle,

and abductors of the leg. Increases flexibility of the
hip joints.

E. EXERCISES FOR THE SHOULDER GIRDLE AND ARMS

1. *Raising and Lowering Shoulders*
   a. *Starting position:* Standing, with feet together and
   arms extended over head.
   b. *Exercise:*
      (1) Lift the right shoulder, letting the chest sink.
      (2) Actively pull the right shoulder blade down and
      into the center of the back. Do the same with the
      left shoulder.
      (3) Alternate the action in the right and left shoul-
      ders, with one raised while the other is pulled
      down.
      (4) Raise both shoulders and pull both shoulders
      down as the neck is stretched upward.
      (5) Concentrate on lifting the sternum as the shoul-
      ders are pulled down.
   c. *Value:* Localizes control of muscle groups producing
   upper back extension and elevation of the sternum.

2. *Knee Bend Push-ups*
   a. *Starting position:* Lying in a prone position, with
   knees bent and feet raised. The elbows are bent and
   palms of hands against the floor under the shoulders.
   b. *Exercise:*
      (1) Tighten the body and push with the arms, raising
      the body off the floor until the elbows are straight.
      (2) Lower the body by bending the elbows.
      (3) Maintain a straight body position from head to
      knees.
   c. *Value:* Strengthens the extensors of the arms; stabilizes the scapulae and pectorals.

3. *Stretch and Double-up*
   a. *Starting position:* Squatting, with the body leaning

forward and the hands placed on the floor below the shoulders.

b. *Exercise:*

   (1) Shoot the legs back so that the body is in a stretched position and in a straight line from head to toes.

   (2) Return to the starting position.

   (3) NOTE: It is necessary momentarily to raise the hips and place the weight on the arms in order to reach the stretch position and return to the starting position. The elbows should be slightly bent and the body should reach the straight position without arching first.

c. *Value:* Strengthens muscles of the shoulder girdle, and extensors of the back and arms.

4. *Nose Dive*

   a. *Starting position:* Standing in a deep-knee-bend position on the left leg, with the right leg extended backward on the floor.

   b. *Exercise:*

      (1) Raise the right leg upward, lean forward with the body, and catch weight on hands as the body falls forward.

      (2) Stretch the elbows, bend them, stretch and bend them again.

      (3) Lower the right leg to the floor, shift the weight to both feet, and return to standing position.

      (4) Repeat with the other leg.

   c. *Value:* Strengthens the muscle of the shoulder girdle, the thigh of the bending leg, and the extensors of the stretched leg.

5. *Stretch and Contract*

   a. *Starting position:* Standing, with the upper body and arms contracted and the feet comfortably apart.

   b. *Exercise:*

     (1) Extend the upper back, arms, and neck directly upward with slow sustained movement. When the maximum extension is reached, return to the contracted position.

     (2) Extend the upper back, arms, and neck diagonally forward left. Return to contracted position.

     (3) Vary the direction of extension to include diagonally forward right, diagonally backward right and left, sideward, backward, and forward.

     (4) Note: The extension may take seven counts and the contraction just one count. Place concentration on the action of extending by degrees and fulfilling the span of time allotted for extension. The knees and pelvis are free to change position.

  c. *Value:* Increases muscle tonus and flexibility in the shoulder girdle and arms. Localizes the action of lifting the sternum.

6. *Arm Swinging*

  a. *Starting position:* Standing, with feet comfortably apart and arms extended sideward.

  b. *Exercise:*

     (1) Swing the arms across the body and out to the sides in a regular swing rhythm.

     (2) Increase the tempo until the swing is fast and requires a great deal of effort.

     (3) Gradually decrease the tempo until the swing is in slow motion.

     (4) Repeat steps one, two, and three with one arm swinging forward while the other arm swings backward.

     (5) Repeat steps one, two, and three with arms swinging horizontally around the body.

  c. *Value:* Increases muscular tonus in the arms, strengthens shoulders, and focuses the attention on movement of the arms.

7. *Arm Vibrations*

    a. *Starting position:* Standing, with feet comfortably apart and arms extended sideward.

    b. *Exercise:*

        (1) Stretch the body and arms, producing as much tension as possible.

        (2) Beat the arms up and down within a very small range; at the same time, resist the up and down motion.

        (3) NOTE: The beating motion is so tight and so small that it appears to be a shivering motion.

    c. *Value:* Increases tension in the muscles of the shoulder girdle and strengthens the levators of the arms.

8. *Shoulder Pull*

    a. *Starting position:* Standing, with feet together and arms extended overhead.

    b. *Exercise:*

        (1) Pull the right shoulder down and back by concentrating on the pull into the center of the back.

        (2) Pull the left shoulder down in the same manner.

        (3) Combine the above movement with a slow walk, completing two shoulder movements to each step.

        (4) NOTE: Maintain high carriage of the sternum and avoid hyperextension in the lower back.

    c. *Value:* Increases muscular tension in the upper back, shoulder girdle, and levators of the arms. Localizes attention in the muscle groups responsible for correct carriage of the shoulders.

9. *Extended Sit-Bounce*

    a. *Starting position:* Sitting, with back straight, legs stretched forward, and arms stretched over the head.

    b. *Exercise:*

        (1) Lean forward from the hips with a straight back, taking a series of twelve very small bounces.

(2) Round the back over the legs, drop the arms, and return to starting position.

c. *Value:* Strengthens the extensors of the back, stabilizes the shoulder girdle, and strengthens the levators of the arms.

10. *Arm Pulling*

a. *Starting position:* Standing, with right arm raised, elbow bent, and palm of hand facing the body. Stand next to partner with right sides together.

b. *Exercise:*

(1) Join right hands.

(2) Lean away from partner but maintain the bent arm position.

(3) Walk in a circle, pulling away from partner.

(4) Change sides and do the same with the left arm.

(5) NOTE: This exercise can be done in a circle formation as in a grand right and left, but complete a whole circle instead of a half circle.

c. *Value:* Increases muscular tension in the flexors of the arm and lateral flexors of the spine.

F. EXERCISES FOR THE FEET

1. *Toe-Heel Walk*

a. *Starting position:* Sitting straight, with knees bent, feet apart and close to the body.

b. *Exercise:*

(1) Grasp the right ankle with the right hand from the inside of the leg. Grasp the left ankle with the left hand in the same manner.

(2) Lift the right heel off the floor and point the toes on the floor.

(3) Lower the heel and bring it forward.

(4) Repeat with the left foot.

(5) Alternate the toe-heel action between the right and left foot.

(6) Release grasp on ankle and alternately reach fo
ward with right toe-heel and left toe-heel, gradu
ally extending legs forward. Walk them back to
starting position.

c. *Value:* Localizes the tension in the gastrocnemius
and plantar flexors responsible for extending the
ankle and pointing the toes.

2. *Ankle Flexion and Extension*
  a. *Starting position:* Sitting upright, with the legs spread
  and arms at sides.
  b. *Exercise:*
  (1) Flex the ankles, letting the knees bend.
  (2) Push from the hips, extend the knees and ankles,
  and press the toes toward the floor.
  (3) NOTE: The extension should be slow enough to
  allow concentration on the muscles producing the
  movement.
  c. *Value:* Increases flexibility of ankle flexors and extensors.

3. *Instep Stretch*
  a. *Starting position:* Standing, with weight on left leg.
  The right leg is bent and rotated outward, and the
  top of the toes rest on the floor.
  b. *Exercise:*
  (1) Gradually shift part of the weight onto the right
  instep.
  (2) Shift the weight back to the left foot. Repeat
  three times.
  (3) Change the weight to the right leg and stretch the
  left instep.
  c. *Value:* Provides an indication of the range of ankle
  extension that is possible when muscle control is sufficient to produce such extension. Requires conscious
  effort in relaxing while stretching.

4. *Heel Raising*
   a. *Starting position:* Standing, with feet together and arms at sides.
   b. *Exercise:*
      (1) Shift the weight forward so that it is centered over the balls of the feet. Maintain an erect body position.
      (2) Rise to the toes, keeping the knees straight.
      (3) Lower the heels. Repeat eleven times.
      (4) NOTE: The weight should be carried through the insteps and big toe. Avoid rolling the ankles outward.
   c. *Value:* Strengthens the gastrocnemius and plantar flexors of the foot.

5. *Beats and Points*
   a. *Starting position:* Standing on the left leg in an outward rotated position, with the right ankle extended forward and pointed.
   b. *Exercise:*
      (1) Quickly bring the right heel to the left toe and point the toe forward again. Repeat seven times. On the last point rotate the leg outward and point directly sideward.
      (2) Bring the heel to the toe and point sideward again. Each time the heel is brought into the left foot it should be placed alternately at the toe and at the heel of the left foot. Repeat the sideward points seven times, ending with the right foot pointing backward.
      (3) Repeat the points, bringing the toes of the right foot to the heel of the left. Keep legs straight throughout the exercise.
      (4) Shift weight to the right foot and repeat the exercise with the other leg.

   c. *Value:* Increases flexibility of ankle extension and provides discipline for accurate foot placement.

6. *Low Walks and Runs*
   a. *Starting position:* Standing in a bent-knee position, with weight inclined forward.
   b. *Exercise:*
     (1) Walk forward, eliminating any vertical motion. Maintain the knee bend position and actively grasp the floor with the feet.
     (2) Weight should be taken on the ball of the foot first and then transferred to the heel and through the bending knee. Walk in slow motion.
     (3) Run in the same position and emphasize the back-leg push and the transfer of weight to the forward leg.
   c. *Value:* Strengthens the extensors of the legs, feet, and hips.

7. *Hopping*
   a. *Starting position:* Standing on the left leg, with right leg raised forward in a bent position.
   b. *Exercise:*
     (1) Bounce on the left leg and gradually increase the elevation until the foot leaves the floor. Gradually diminish the hop back to a knee bounce.
     (2) Shift weight to the right leg and repeat the exercise. The exercise on one foot should continue for sixteen counts.
     (3) NOTE: The ankle action should be as follows: On elevation, the hip and knee straightens, heel rises, toes rise; on landing, toes land, heels land, knee and hip joints bend.
   c. *Value:* Strengthens the extensors of the leg, feet, and hips, and improves balance.

8. *Jumps*
   a. *Starting position:* Standing in first position (see page 72), with arms at sides.
   b. *Exercise:*
      (1) Jump eight times, concentrating on controlling the elevation and landing and maintaining the leg position when off the ground.
      (2) Jump eight times in second position.
      (3) Jump eight times, alternating from first to second.
      (4) Jump eight times in fifth position, changing the feet so that the left foot is in front on the odd counts and the right foot is in front on the even.
      (5) Note: The body should remain straight at all times. Take special care to avoid bending forward on landing.
   c. *Value:* Strengthens extensors of the hips, legs, and feet.

9. *Position jumps:*
   a. *Starting position:* Standing in first position (see page 72).
   b. *Exercise:*
      (1) Jump eight times in first position.
      (2) Change the leg position on each jump during the elevated phase; heels together, legs spread sideward, both knees bent forward, one leg forward and one backward.
   c. *Value:* Strengthens extensors of hips, legs, and feet.

10. *Jump turn*
    a. *Starting position:* Standing in first position (see page 72).
    b. *Exercise:*
       (1) Jump three times in first position.
       (2) Make one complete turn on the fourth jump. Land in a plié facing front and hold balance.

     (3) Repeat the jumps, and turn in the opposite direction.

  c. *Value:* Strengthens extensors of hips, legs, and feet. feet, and increases muscular tonus in the spinal rotators.

The dancer's needs are many. She needs an agile and well-controlled body—one which is flexible and yet has enough strength and muscle tension to do strong and quick movements and to adjust to various qualities of movement readily. She needs speed of action and reaction, efficiency and economy of muscle action, a fine kinesthetic awareness of degrees of muscular relaxation and tension, and a sense of position in space. Such physical adequacy is indispensable to a sense of security.

The conditioning program can yield these values if it is properly taught. The conditioning part of dance education should be an awakening period in which the student learns what the body is capable of doing under intelligent direction. This period should be one of discovery and understanding of the basic principles of the structure and function of the body as well as a period of physical skill development.

These principles should be carried over and applied to the lessons on fundamental movement experiences. The conditioning part of a lesson is aimed at emphasizing particular structural and functional principles that are related to movement. One note of caution must be injected here. The conditioning program is not intended to precede the teaching of fundamental movement experiences as a unit but rather constitutes a part of those lessons. The conditioning program should go hand in hand with creative activity, since each is a functional part of the other. The reasons for placing conditioning exercises at the beginning of this chapter are stated in Chapter 8.

3

Fundamental
Movement
Experiences

The first, and very important, objective in teaching dance is to develop basic control of the large muscle groups, so that the individual has a foundation on which to develop further. Control of the body is a result of muscular efficiency. This efficiency is developed through consistent and co-ordinated use of large muscle groups according to basic functional principles of movement. These principles must become a regular part of the student's movement habits so that she uses them reflexly.

First, the student must find correct vertical stance. In order to do this she must learn to contract the abdominal and gluteal muscles and at the same time pull the shoulder blades down and into the center of the back. This co-ordination seems to be difficult to achieve, since the average student leans backward from the waist to the neck. She usually feels that she is on an incline forward when she is actually standing straight and in correct alignment. It is necessary for the student to adjust her understanding and kinesthetic awareness of what she thought was a straight position to coincide with correct vertical stance. This adjustment comes through constant practice in moving into such a position, becoming aware of how it feels.

Second, the student must learn to use the legs and feet properly in locomotion. She must learn to grasp the floor with the foot in transferring weight, carry the hips over the ball of the foot, and then push out of the floor by extending the leg. She can achieve this by contracting the gluteals, thigh, and calf, and following through with the ankle and toes so that the action travels continuously throughout the leg from the hip through the toes. On landing, she should reach for the floor with just the reverse action. The ball of the foot makes contact first, the heel is lowered to the floor, the knee bends, and the thigh and gluteals contract in order to break the fall and produce a light landing. The co-ordination and timing of this action must become smooth so that the body is lowered to the floor without shock or strain on any part. The upper part of the body must be related tensionally to the rest of the body and should be stretched to resist gravity both in elevation and landing. For most students, extensive practice is necessary to achieve such control.

Third, the student must learn to initiate peripheral movement—that is, movement of the arms and legs from the center of the body. Actually, all movement is initiated in the body, even though this is often not obvious. Arm and leg movements should be extensions of movement initiated in the body and thus bear a relationship to the body position and tension. (This, of course, excludes purposeful isolated movement that is intentional and not the result of lack of control.)

Fourth, the student must learn to find her center of balance in a variety of positions. This she learns by shifting her weight on one leg and becoming aware of the necessary compensation in the hip. If she wants to balance on one leg, she shifts her center of gravity over one leg and maintains a hip position that is centered over the standing base and is parallel to the floor (avoiding passive hanging against the hip joint). She should experiment with movement in this position and learn to recognize the difference between active and passive balancing. The student must find her balance kinesthetically in different dimensions, with the body in off-center positions, on different levels, and in locomotion.

Fifth, the student must learn to move rhythmically in a well-co-ordinated manner. The well-co-ordinated student naturally moves rhythmically. The poorly co-ordinated student who disciplines herself by moving rhythmically will find co-ordination much easier, except where emotional conflicts hamper her.

The following fundamental lessons constitute an application of the principles stated above. These lessons are far from conclusive; rather, they are here to serve as examples. The over-all progression is from large to small muscle groups and from movement in the central part of the body to movement of the extremities. This plan is followed because human beings in the process of development and maturation follow this pattern naturally. Without total body control, movement of the extremities cannot be properly executed, for control of the extremities is dependent on central control in the body as a whole.

The application of principles of movement are provided for in the lessons that follow. Little obvious use of rhythm is found in the form of the lesson plans because it is assumed that it will be developed through the constant use of the various kinds of rhythm which should be present in all lessons. Furthermore, it is an impossibility to teach movement efficiently without rhythmic organization. Rhythm is a part of everything that one does in movement. If the teacher sets the movement, she should organize it rhythmically. If she organizes movement produced by the student, she should take its natural rhythm and set it so that it is definite and accurate. If the class is moving across the floor four counts apart, she should emphasize this organization so that each group comes in at the right time; if a class fails to grasp rhythm kinesthetically, she should analyze the principles of rhythmic movement for them. A keen sense of rhythm is developed through consistent and accurate use of rhythmically organized movement. More often than not, students who fail to move rhythmically lack self-discipline in overcoming lethargy, or they are under some emotional stress which blocks normal functioning. The problem is often one of lack of readiness to move at the given pace. The great majority of students, however, develop a sense of rhythm as a result of the rhythmic organization which prevails throughout each lesson.

The following lessons are designed so that the student may become aware of movement and may discover movement principles along with the development of an understanding of the means for controlling and exploring movement. In the early dance experience, the student should learn essentially by exploration. This exploration should lead directly into the development of motor and visual imagery and associations. It is a period of searching for the relationship between movement and expression. The results of such experiences will provide a more adequate foundation for pursuing creative work more directly.

The exercises that are given at the beginning of the following lesson plans have a definite relationship to the development of the lessons. It is assumed that general "warmup" exercises are given at the beginning of each lesson, so they have not been included in the following lesson plans. Release activities may or may not be needed at the end of a lesson; their use or nonuse will depend on the lesson and the class.

Probably the most important immediate objectives for the teacher to strive to attain with a beginning group are the following: (1) to stimulate the individual to move, (2) to provide experiences through which the student can develop a love for controlled freedom in movement, (3) to stimulate curiosity about movement which will be satisfied through experimentation and will lead to creative discovery of movement-idea relationships, (4) to reduce inhibitions and physical insecurity, (5) to develop the ability to move as a total unit and direct the body intelligently, through an understanding of fundamental principles of movement.

Fundamental Movement Experience: Contractions and extensions, with variation in level, rhythm, quality, contrast, and locomotion.

PROBLEM 1

A. *Lying on back:*

1. Straight contraction: contract the abdominal muscles, causing the lower back to be pressed to the floor while the head and shoulders are lifted off the floor. Arms are at the sides and off the floor. Lower the shoulders and head to the floor, maintaining the abdominal contraction while bringing the arms overhead on the floor; pull the shoulder girdle down and into the center of the back while stretching the neck, and maintain the abdominal contraction throughout; release all tension and bring arms to sides again. Repeat.

   a. The tendency on lowering the body to the floor is to collapse, and this should be avoided. It should be a lengthening contraction.

   b. In cases where an individual has difficulty pulling the shoulders down toward the lower back, have her lift the chest off the floor and arch the back. Once the action is localized, combine it with the abdominal contraction.

2. Diagonal contraction: contract diagonally, pulling the right shoulder toward the left thigh. The contraction should be initiated in the abdominal muscles; the greatest tension exists in the center of the body; avoid rolling to one side. Return to the lying position again, fixing the hips and pulling shoulder blades down toward the center of the back.

3. Side contractions: contract on one side of the body, causing the upper body to be pulled laterally toward the legs on the same side; the body remains flat on the floor. Return to a straight lying position. Repeat on the other side.

B. *Exploration*

1. Using the straight, diagonal, and side contractions with alternate extensions, have the group start in a lying position and experiment with the number of different ways they may contract and be aware of the resulting position. After each contraction, which raises the body to a slightly higher level, have the students extend in whatever position they are in and maintain that level; follow that extension with a different contraction which progressively brings them to a higher position. Let them explore as many different contractions as they can find on each level until they reach an upright position. Then have them work downward again. Set a definite number of counts within which they must complete each contraction and extension.

   a. Emphasize the fact that contracting with gravity is not the same as relaxing into a bent position.

   b. Point out some interesting positions as you see them.

   c. Have the group attempt to remember each position they are in so they may become kinesthetically aware of how the different positions feel; this will aid them in finding those positions again.

2. Do the same progressions as in B-1, varying the quality of movement by:

   a. Contracting for four counts and extending on one count.

   b. Doing the same progression in slow motion.

   c. Doing both contraction and extension percussively, using one count for each.

   d. Doing the whole progression with one continuous contraction after another, eliminating the extension.

C. *Locomotion*

1. From a standing position, take a sudden contraction into a crouched position. Follow this with a sustained

extension, leaning straight from the ankles. Continue stretching until it is necessary to run in the direction of the extension to catch oneself. Repeat across the floor.

2. Traveling on a fast running base, gradually uncurl from a rounded body position to a full extension.

3. Repeat C-1 and add a series of fast contractions, one after another, which progressively lower the body to the floor. Resume the progression of alternate contraction and extension on getting up from the floor and continue running to the end of the room.

D. *The student should experience:*

1. Tension in the center of the body as a controlling basis for all movement.

2. Different balance points for each new position.

3. The relationship of tension in the extremities to contractive and extensive movement in the body.

4. The extremes in range of movement in a variety of positions.

5. Principles of active lowering of the body to the floor and lifting from the floor.

6. Movement in a variety of positions and dimensions with kinesthetic awareness of how they feel.

7. Exploration of various body positions with awareness of feeling states.

8. The importance of co-ordinating contraction and extension of different parts of the body in controlling and directing movement.

Fundamental Movement Experience: Chest lift and suspension in carriage of the upper body.

PROBLEM 2

A. *Lying position*

1. *On back:* lift the chest off the floor, allowing the head to hang back. Repeat many times.

2. *Prone:* bend the knees and grasp the feet over the insteps with the hands. Push lower legs back while pulling against them with the arms; this results in lifting the upper body and legs off the floor. Stretch upward with the neck; keep the hips on the floor; release.

3. *Prone:* stretch the arms sideward in a T position; lift the upper back, head, and arms toward the ceiling simultaneously; counteract the action of peeling off the floor by tightening the abdominal muscles to make an extreme arch in the lower back.

B. *Standing*

1. Let the body hang forward from the hips, with the knees bent. Gradually straighten upward by uncurling the body to a straight position, starting at the lower end of the spine and traveling upward toward the head. The student should become aware of keeping the weight centered over the metatarsals, stabilizing the hips as she straightens, and getting the back in straight alignment. The shoulders should be depressed and chest lifted as the upper back is straightened.

2. Most people habitually lean back from the waist, and consequently, when they are aligned properly, they feel that they are falling forward. Therefore, they must develop a new concept of what straight alignment is.

C. *Locomotion*

1. From a standing position, assume a crouched position with the knees bent. Starting with a slow walk, gradually increase the tempo until it becomes a run. At the same time, gradually uncurl the body until it is straight.

2. Take a four count run in an upright position, getting a forward lean from the ankles. Jump into the crouched position on counts 5 and 6, come to a full extension and suspend on the toes on counts 7 and 8.

Repeat. (It is necessary to pull the legs under the hips on the jump to check the forward motion.)

3. Repeat the sequence in number 2 and add the problem of getting to the floor and up again without breaking the continuity of movement. This is more exciting when improvised rather than planned. The sequence would be: run for four counts, jump into a crouched position, extend the body to a suspension, lower the body to the floor through a series of contractions, and come up again. A definite number of counts should be set within which the student must complete her sequence of getting to the floor and up again. The number of counts taken for the whole phrase should be determined by the average level of ability of the class. By watching the class go through the sequence once, the teacher can determine how many counts are needed.

4. Divide the class in half, with one group at each end of the room. Have each line execute the sequence in number 2 and attempt to synchronize their timing as groups. Have each group move on opposing diagonals, coming toward the middle of the room. On each repetition of the sequence, the opposite diagonal should be used. The groups should try to relate their movement to those they meet and become aware of the opposing tensional pull as they suspend and pass each other (see Figure 1).

D. *Students should experience:*

1. Localization of upper back extension and kinesthetic awareness of the lift through the chest which it fosters.

2. A sense of importance in the proper carriage of the chest in all movement, whether contracting, extending, or lowering the body to the floor and lifting it up again.

3. Suspension of the body through the chest lift in its natural timing.

4. Suspension of the body at its highest point before a drop in relation to an opposition group movement.
5. The feeling of attractive force relating groups moving in opposition to each other.
6. Improvisation from an off-balance suspension into a fall and recovery.

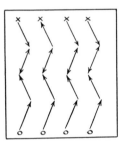

Figure 1.

Fundamental Movement Experience: Tensional relationships.

PROBLEM 3

A. *Explanation:* tensional relationship refers to the attractive force which relates the movement of one person to another person or one group to another group. When they are related tensionally, they appear as a total unit. This involves the process of setting up points of resistance against which one moves parts of the body, thus giving movement direction and a particular degree of tension.

B. *Procedure:*
1. Have each student take a partner about her own size Have them join right hands and face each other.
2. The couples should move in any way possible but re sist the pull of each other. They may change their grip in order to be in another position but should not drop their tension in the process. They may move parallel or in opposition to each other.

3. The resistance should be muscular rather than simply a leaning with dead weight, and the pull between the two should be equalized in order to avoid falling or collapsing off balance.

4. After sufficient experimentation with this problem, have them set and memorize the sequence of movements they have worked out.

5. After the sequences are set, assign the problem of doing their sequence with the same tensional relationships without holding on to a partner. They must set up the tension in the body to produce the same effect without the aid of outside force.

6. Have each couple perform their study and have the class evaluate them. Point out the effects of design formed by the various positions of the body.

C. *The student should experience:*

1. Tensional relationships formed within her own body and those in relation to another person.

2. An understanding of the process of points of resistance against which one works to produce such degrees of tension.

3. An understanding of the principles of movement design.

4. Kinesthetic awareness of movement responses between oneself and another person.

5. Kinesthetically and visually the sculptural effect of bodies related in movement design and an awareness of accompanying feeling states.

Fundamental Movement Experience: Arm movement related to the body.

PROBLEM 4

A. *Explanation:* one of the most difficult skills for the beginner to acquire is that of getting tension into arm movement. The beginner just does not know how to set up tension in the arms. One means of attacking this problem is by using a prop which aids the student in setting up tension in the arms. It also establishes a tensional relationship between the arms and the body.

B. *Procedure*

1. Provide the students with a piece of rope, cotton cloth, or even a belt from a dress. The rope or other item used should be approximately one yard in length.
2. Experiment with the rope by holding it at various lengths and pulling on each end. There should be adequate strength in the pull to produce action.
3. Let the tension and pull of the arms cause the body to change position.
4. The student should strive to move with the whole body in the same tensional relationship and should experiment with many different ways of moving the arms and changing the body positions.
5. Have the students work out a sequence of changes which builds in interest and uses contrast in movement quality and rhythm.
6. Have the students rework the sequence without the rope, trying to produce the same quality of movement.

C. *Students should experience:*

1. New ways of moving.
2. New relationships of arm movement to body positions.
3. Kinesthetic awareness of tensional pull in arm movement.
4. Spatial awareness of the sculptural aspect of movement when all parts of the body are related in movement.
5. Form in arm movement with and without the aid of of a prop.
6. An understanding of the process of producing tension in arm movement.

Fundamental Movement Experience: Movement in a curved path.

PROBLEM 5

A. *Explanation:* Movement in a curved path which is well directed and accurate provides unlimited possibilities for expression. Utilization of curved movement not only adds interest to exploration because of its never-ending nature, but also insures against the stereotyped and angular movement so typical of beginners. (For analysis of movement in a curved path, see page 76.)

B. *Procedure:*

1. In a standing position with the right hand pointing to the floor, move that arm in a figure-eight motion, initiating the movement from the shoulder. Experiment with the figure eight by executing the movement in as many different planes around the body as one can find. After the circular action is well established, let the body describe the same motion as the arm. Move from one place to another with the same action. Do the same with the other arm.

2. Leading with the palm of the hand as the pressure point, make a figure eight which spirals from down below the hips and travels up and over the head. Do the same action in the body. Do the same on the other side.

3. Standing with feet slightly apart, swing the hips from one side, through a curve to the back, and over to the other side; swing the hips in a complete circle, with knees bending as needed. Practice swinging the hips in both directions all around the circle. Step the circle out with the feet while swinging the hips in a circular path.

4. Start at one corner of the room(T) (Figure 2). Run in a large semi-circle the length of the room and end

up in the opposite corner(Z), directly in line with the starting point. When one moves in a circular path, it is necessary to lean toward the center around which one is moving(O); one should feel traction toward this center. The curve should be gradual and smooth.

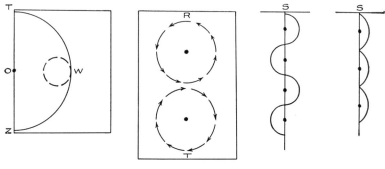

Figure 2.   Figure 3.   Figure 4.   Figure 5.

5. Vary number four by adding a small circle at W(Figure 2). One should get into the small circle and come out of it without breaking the continuity of the curve.
6. If the gym floor has two circles on it, use them for this problem. Starting at R(Figure 3), run on the circle counterclockwise, always leaning toward the center. When the first half circle is almost completed, follow the tangent off the first circle and go into the second circle, leaning toward the center of that circle; complete that circle and follow the tangent into the first circle, again shifting to lean toward the center of that circle. Have students begin the above sequence four counts or eight runs apart so that many people will be moving at once. The students will develop a sense of moving in a curved path more rapidly when they are part of large group motion. Try starting half the

group at R(Figure 3) and the other half at T(Figure 3), with individuals starting at four count intervals. They should maintain equal distance from each other in order to cross from one circle to the next without breaking the rhythm.

7. Moving in a single file down the floor, imagine a straight line around which one moves in a semi-circle (Figure 4). Set a definite number of counts. If one takes four counts to get around the curve and two to collect herself, the two counts can be utilized for emphasis on shift of the body in relation to the center. If an individual moves through the pattern of Figure 4, she starts with a lean to the right center (the dot in each figure represents the center toward which one leans). When that curve is finished, she must shift her weight to lean toward left center in order to progress through space. If one follows Figure 5, the first curve is taken moving forward on the curve with a right lean, and the second is taken moving backward on the curve with a left lean to center. In order to be accurate and to experience true curved motion, one must relate the side of her body to the center and be careful not to twist the upper to partially face the center.

C. *Students should experience:*
  1. The difference between straight and curved movement.
  2. Centrifugal force in movement.
  3. Sensation of the body moving through a curved path.
  4. Continuity in curved movement.
  5. The traction to a center when executing movement in a curved path.
  6. A new sense of movement through space.
  7. New ways of moving the body.
  8. The effect of weight transference when moving in a curved path.

Fundamental Movement Experience: Carriage in relation to movement quality, projection in space, and feeling states.

PROBLEM 6
A. *Lying in prone position:*
 1. Extend arms overhead on the floor; lift the shoulders, back, arms, and head upward; lower to the floor.
 2. Roll over slowly, initiating the roll by pulling the right shoulder toward the back. Resist in the hips until it is necessary to go all the way over, ending in a back lying position. Repeat until students can localize the action.
B. *Standing:*
 1. In stride position with body rounded forward from the hips, take four relaxed bounces and raise the trunk to a straight position parallel to the floor and hold.
 2. With feet together in upright position and arms overhead, pull both shoulder blades down into the center of the back and stretch the neck upward. Raise the shoulders. Repeat until students can isolate the upper back action and at the same time maintain proper body alignment with stabilized hips.
 3. Repeat number two, alternating right and left.
 4. Drop forward and shake out arms, back, and neck.
C. *Locomotion:*
 1. Take a two count plié, transferring the weight on the first count and straightening the knee on count 2 (very slow tempo).
 2. Repeat number 1 while pulling shoulders down into the center of the back twice to each plié. The hips should be carried over the forward leg; rocking in the hips should be avoided as one transfers her weight.
 3. Walk four counts forward with arms raised to the sides. Raise arms forward slowly while going into lunge (for 2 counts). Come out of the plié using 2 counts,

and improvise arm movement of sustained quality for four counts. Repeat from beginning.

4. Experiment with the use of one arm pulling into the back or across the body, causing the body to move in a curved path. Start with an impulse in the shoulder and follow through with movement that naturally carries out the line of action from the initial pull.

5. Discuss the quality of the movement the students have been doing. Write descriptive terms on the board. Have them consciously use the ideas which come from the group. The essential quality which arises from sustained movement combined with carriage is that of the stately classical dances such as the pavanne. There are a number of English and French suites of classical dance forms available both in sheet music and on recording.

6. Select a recording that is appropriate, or sheet music if an accompanist is available, and improvise to it. Emphasis should be placed on regal quality, dignity, carriage, and design of movement. Let the students improvise freely and in small groups. The problem confronting the student technically is one of moving in a slow and continuous manner, relating movement of the extremities to body movement.

7. One could follow up the development of the resultant ideas through the pre-classic dance forms. For further information, see Louis Horst's [1] book on pre-classic forms.

D. *Students should experience:*

1. Isolation of movement of the shoulder girdle and the co-ordination of stabilizing the pelvis and shoulder girdle to get the proper vertical stance with correct carriage of the chest.

2. The above as a basis for control of extremities in movement.

[1] *Pre-Classic Dance Forms.* New York: The Dance Observer, 1937.

3. A sustained quality of movement and some association of its form with an expressive idea.
4. A sense of carriage and dignity in sustaining movement.
5. An awareness of the sculptural aspect of movement and its projection in space.

Fundamental Movement Experience: Plié and positions related to locomotion, elevation, and image association.

PROBLEM 7

A. *Standing:*

1. Slow pliés in all positions with maximum tension, using two counts for bending and two for extending. Keep the movement continuous (for analysis of plié and positions, see pages 72, 73).
2. Take a four count plié in first, second, and third positions, followed by four steps in the direction indicated by the leg positions. Repeat each position once, taking the alternate directions; that is: first position, move forward; first position, move backward; second position, move right sideward; second, move left sideward; third position, move diagonally forward right; third, move diagonally backward left.
3. Jump: From a first position plié, take a small preparation, push out of the floor and straighten the legs on elevation of the body; extend the body as it leaves the ground and carry weight evenly between legs.
   a. The straightening of the legs, hips, and ankles is almost simultaneous while the body is stretched upward; the gluteals and abdominal muscles are tightly contracted.
   b. Carriage of the body in elevation is best produced by a combination of proper timing in muscle action and psychological motivation. Elevation is done with the body as well as with the legs.

c. To land properly from elevation, it is necessary to reach for the floor and actively grasp the floor with the feet in order to break the fall successively by taking the weight first on the ball of the foot and then by continuous action of bending the ankles and knees and tightening the gluteals. At the same time the body should stretch upward, resisting the fall. One should never relax into the floor on landing from elevation.

4. Prance: stand on the left leg with the right leg lifted forward with a bent knee and the toes pointing to the floor. Press the raised leg into the floor with toes reaching first, heels next, followed by the straightening of the leg and gripping in the gluteals and thigh. As the raised leg presses into the floor, the weight is transferred and the standing leg is then raised. The raised leg and instep presses forward with the fully extended ankle in a position directly under the knee. The standing leg remains straight. Prance at a slow tempo until the co-ordination and awareness of all parts of the action are established. Increase the tempo without making the movement smaller.

B. *Locomotion:*

1. Take four jumps in first position, progressing forward, and change to eight prances. Vary the direction of the jumps by taking them in a sequence of forward, side, back, side, and prance eight forward with emphasis on a quick rebound. The jumps must travel in the above-stated directions. After the class has experienced the sequence, ask for images or ideas they associated with the movement form. Use the ideas and have the class motivate their movement with these ideas or images. They are free to vary the jumps and body positions.

2. Take a combination of jumping from two feet and landing on one foot.

3. Take three patterns of the above. On the landing of the third unit, go down to the floor, tucking the free leg under and getting the body into a doubled-up position; roll over and come up into an elevated position, landing on both feet. The transition from elevation to the floor should be left for the student to work out in her own way.

C. *Students should experience:*
   1. Kinesthetic awareness of the fundamental co-ordination which produces efficient elevation.
   2. An understanding of leg positions and pliés as fundamental preparation for all types of elevation and of their relationship to the direction in which the movement travels.
   3. The difference between movement which is mechanical and that which has motivation.
   4. An association of ideas and images which are aroused by the particular form the movements take.
   5. An understanding of the principles of elevation which the student can use as a measuring device for improvement of her own skill.
   6. A sense of dynamics through contrast in tempo, range, and level of movement.

Fundamental Movement Experience: Exploration of movement quality.

PROBLEM 8
   A. *Standing:*
      1. Swinging quality: take one arm and swing it freely. Get as much relaxation as possible. Emphasize the force of dropping the arm and let it swing through until it reaches a suspension point and is ready to drop again. When the swing is established:
         a. Add the other arm and let the body weight move with the swing.

  b. Let the force of the swing cause the body to move.
  c. Ask the class to describe how the movement feels;
     sum up the characteristics of a swing: (1) the great-
     est amount of force is on the drop or collapse; (2)
     momentum carries movement through an arc which
     is always present in swinging movement; (3) a sus-
     pension is experienced as the arm reaches its high-
     est point before dropping; (4) the natural rhythm
     of a swing is %.
2. Experiment with the same swinging movement by
   slowing the speed of the swing.
  a. Note the way the quality of movement changes.
  b. Ask students to describe the difference in feeling
     between a true swing and the same movement per-
     formed twice as slow.
  c. Question the quality of movement which resulted;
     what would they call it if they were giving it a
     name?
3. Take the same swing, speed up the tempo, and execute
   the same movement in one count.
  a. It necessitates using much more muscular force in
     a short time; there is usually a reduction in the
     size of the movement.
  b. Ask for descriptive terms of how this movement
     differed from the last two variations. How would
     the quality of this movement be described?
4. Take the same movement and reduce it gradually in
   size and increase the speed until it is so fast and so
   small that it appears to be shivering.
  a. Ask for observations on how it felt.
  b. What other movement is closely related to it?
  c. What caused it to be what it is?
  d. What would it be called?
B. *Students should experience:*
  1. The effect of force and time on determining the qual-
     ity of movement.

2. Swinging, percussive, sustained, and vibratory movement, learning to identify them as a result of movement experience.

3. Practice in attending to the feeling of movement and in attempting to describe their feelings verbally or by analogy.

4. An understanding of factors of time and force which condition different qualities of movement.

Fundamental Movement Experience: Locomotion.

PROBLEM 9

A. *Standing:*

1. Prancing: the body should be erect. Raise the right knee forward with the ankle extended and toes pointing to the floor. Press the right foot into the floor as the left knee is raised to the starting position of the right leg. The ball of the foot presses into the floor followed by the heel and a straightening of the knee. Avoid sitting into the hips by gripping in the gluteals. Emphasis should be placed on the upward lift of the body in resisting gravity. The common fault is settling with gravity rather than resisting it.

2. With the feet slightly apart and straight ahead, bend the knees and hips as far as possible, keeping the heels on the floor. Straighten hips, knees, and ankles; this results in rising to the toes. Start at a very slow tempo and increase it gradually. As the tempo gets faster, push harder until the body leaves the floor. Emphasize full extension of legs from hips to toes. Straight carriage of the body should be maintained without collapsing or bending the body on landing. During elevation the body should be kept in a straight vertical line.

B. *Locomotion:*

1. Prancing forward: concentrate on keeping a steady

pulse in the bounce and getting smooth action on elevation and landing.

2. Add to number 1 a change of direction at any desired point.

3. Change the body position from vertical to inclined forward and continue the same action in the legs. This results in a run (the body lean on a forward run should be a degree of incline which is optimal for getting a continued driving force with the legs so that the body rushes through space with vitality). Let the group start from a leaning position forward and have the accompanist pick up a tempo which is comfortable for a run. When the action of landing is good, increase the tempo.

4. Apply more force on the push-off, with a moderate incline forward which should elevate the body higher. Emphasize the transfer of weight in the air with the hips riding on top of the extended leg. The gluteals must be actively contracted both on the take-off and landing in order to get off the floor and avoid sitting in the hips on the landing.

5. Running backwards: reach with the leg from the hip. Get the same grasping action as in the forward run. The body should have a slight lean backward, but not enough to cause the body to be on the verge of falling.

6. Combine forward and backward running, changing after eight, then four, and then two runs.

7. In groups of two to five, work out a sequence of running, leaping, and bouncing movement with rhythmic contrast and directional changes. All movement of a group is to be in unison.

C. *Students should experience:*

1. Practice in co-ordinated use of legs and body in basic locomotion.

2. Kinesthetic awareness of the total body in action while executing locomotion.

3. A sense of rhythmic accuracy and awareness of direction in unison group movement.
4. An understanding of how efficient locomotion is produced.

Fundamental Movement Experience: Accent and syncopation.

PROBLEM 10

A. *Standing:*
 1. With the body normally relaxed and the knees slightly bent, take a constant small bounce, going down on the beat and up after the beat in a regular $\frac{2}{4}$ rhythm.
 2. Shift the weight from one foot to the other after every two counts and then on every count.
 3. Jump in place on the primary accent of a $\frac{4}{4}$ meter. Walk in place for the next three counts. At the same time keeping going the bounce that was established in number 1.

B. *Locomotion:*
 1. Move forward through space, using a step for the accented beats and a hop for the unaccented beats. Start with the accent on the first beat of a $\frac{4}{4}$ measure. The second time through, accent the second beat, then the third, and then the fourth.
 2. Using the same locomotor steps, place the step on the second and fourth beats and the hop on the first and third beats.
 3. Repeat exercise two with a partner; one student takes the accents as stated and the other student maintains a constant pattern of one step and three hops.
 4. Walk forward, stepping on the first and third counts and rising on the toes on the second and fourth counts. Add an accented movement with the arms and body on counts two and four. Alternate this pattern with three steps and an accented jump on count four.

5. Standing in place with the weight on the left foot, tap the right foot in front and raise the knee immediately; leap onto the foot that was tapped. Repeat the same with the right leg. The tap is done on count one and three and the leap on count two and four. The rhythm must be kept even. This is achieved by consuming as much time for the tap as the leap.
6. After the tap-leap pattern is established, move through space with it (see *turns*, page 81).
7. Do the tap-leap on a turning base.

C. *Students should experience:*

1. Kinesthetic and motor response to rhythm.
2. Rhythmic accuracy through responding in movement to accented meter.
3. An understanding of the principle of syncopation.
4. Movement control through rhythmic accuracy.
5. The effect that rhythmic organization exerts on movement in giving it form and clarity.
6. A kinesthetic awareness of the quality and feeling which is a distinct part of syncopated movement.

Further consideration of fundamental movement principles

A. *Direction:*

Body direction exists as a result of movement that is projected through space. The body may move forward, sideward, backward, diagonally right forward, diagonally right backward, diagonally left forward, diagonally left backward, up, down, and in a circle.

In order to produce these directions, the body must move in the above-stated directions while it is facing directly forward in reference to the room. When movement is subjected to directional discipline it becomes more definite and more clearly stated. When movement is oriented in definite directions, the contrast of one movement to another increases in strength. Through such discipline the individual defines her relationship to space. This process is necessary if she wishes to communicate her idea clearly.

Spatial direction, on the other hand, is based on an organization of working space. If an individual stands in the center of the room, the space directly in front of her is forward; the space to each side of her is sideward; the space midway between forward and sideward is diagonally forward; the space midway between sideward and backward is diagonally backward; the space above is up; the space below is down; and the space around the body is circular. The student must become familiar and aware of spatial direction and body direction. When the individual maintains a forward direction in the body and a forward direction in space, she may move in any direction, and the body and space directions will coincide. On the other hand, the body may be directed forward and moved on a diagonal in space simply by turning the body to face the diagonal of the room. The student may direct the body sideward and move in a forward direction in space by making a quarter turn so that her side is facing the front of the room. If she now moves in that position toward the front of the room, she is moving sideward in a forward spatial direction. If one thinks in terms of lines arising from the body and projecting through space, as in Figure 6, the organization of body and spatial direction becomes clear.

The most troublesome problem connected with body and space directions is that of the diagonal. The diagonal body direction is a line which divides the forward and sideward directions in half. It is a 45° angle. In order to move on a spatial diagonal with a diagonal direction in the body, one must travel in fourth position. The body must be facing directly front while moving on the diagonal. If a turn out in the legs is not used, the hips turn in the direction of the diagonal and the direction becomes either forward in the body or halfway between diagonal and forward, and the body orientation in space is poorly defined.

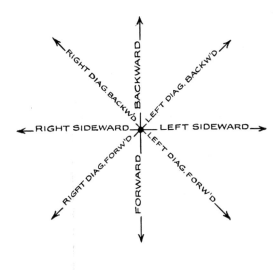

Figure 6.

Movement that is subjected to clarification of direction immediately becomes clearer and more cleanly executed. Movement not accurately directed forward or diagonally or to the side is only an approximation of these directions and invariably lacks clarity. If students understand the function of body and spatial direction in movement, they will become aware of applying these principles while they create movement, and they will do a more adequate job of communication.

B. *Positions:*

If the student wishes to make body and spatial direction coincide, she must move accurately in all directions while the body faces forward in space. In order to execute movement in these directions, the student must utilize outward rotation in the legs. Following is an analysis of the six leg positions used in modern dance. These positions are similar to ballet but are not identical.

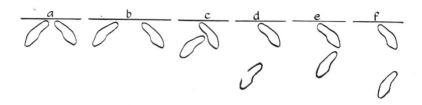

Figure 7. Positions with the right leg taking the changes.

1. *First position:* (a) heels are together, forming a 90° angle. The legs are turned out from the hips. The knees are aligned directly over the metatarsals. The weight is centered between both feet.
2. *Second position:* (b) from first position, extend one leg directly sideward and shift the weight until it is centered between both legs. Retain the same degree of outward rotation as in the first positon.
3. *Third position:* (c) shift the weight to the right leg and bring the left heel to the right instep at a 90° angle. Distribute weight evenly on both feet.
4. *Fourth position:* (d) from third position extend the left foot diagonally forward left and shift the weight evenly between both legs.
5. *Fifth position:* (e) bring the left heel to the toes of the right foot; the left leg and foot is still on the left forward diagonal. Distribute the weight evenly on both feet.
6. *Sixth position:* (f) extend the left foot forward, maintaining the outward rotation in the hips. Center the weight between both feet. The following points apply to all positions:
   a. The turn out from the hips must be maintained not only when one arrives at a position but at all times in the transition from one position to another.
   b. The weight must be divided equally between both feet in all positions.
   c. The body must be facing squarely to the front with no twisting in the hips.

C. *Pliés:*

Pliés accomplish two main purposes: first, they require concentrated effort and muscular tension, which results in heightening of kinesthetic awareness in addition to the development of leg control; second, through habitual practice of pliés the student is prepared for all types of elevation, landing, and locomotion in any direction. However, pliés are of value only if they are done correctly. Pliés are knee bends that are done in a particular way. They are done in the six positions as previously described. The bend should be initiated in the thigh muscles which set up resistance to the outward pull. At the same time, the knees are forced outward. As a result of the outward pull, the body is lowered. During the process of bending, the body should be stretched upward against the outward pull of the legs. In other words, a two-way stretch is produced —upward in a vertical dimension with the body and outward in a horizontal dimension with the legs. The projection of the body is forward in the depth dimension.

During the straightening phase of the plié, the body is continually stretched upward, and the knees straighten while the resistance to the straightening of the knees is maintained. The student should continue straightening the knees until both legs are entirely straight and tight. There is no relaxation period during the bending or stretching or during the transition from one position to another.

D. *Movement through a curved path:*

Movement through a curved path is probably one of the most difficult skills to master. Too often it is confused with describing a circular floor pattern. One can describe a circular floor pattern and fail to execute movement through a curved path.

When one moves in a true curved path the body maintains the same relationship to its central axis at all times. The body direction necessarily changes constantly in order to maintain a constant relationship to its central axis. The body direction is forward in relation to the spatial direction of the curve.

Movement Through a Curved Path

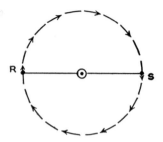

Figure 8. Finding a central axis in movement through a curved path.
R and S are students moving through a curved path attached to student
O as the central axis.

One of the simplest ways of experiencing movement through
a curved path with a stationary axis is to have three students
work together; one student pivots in place as the axis around
which the other two students move. The student in the center
spreads her arms sideward and grasps the hand of each student.
The students on the outside lean slightly away from center
with the shoulders and toward center with the hips so that they
feel a pulling force toward the center as they walk or run
through a circle around the center student. The sideline of
the body is related to the central axis by a straight line which is
constant. The body is thus kept in a forward position in relation to the circle through which it travels. If the body were not
constantly changing direction, the movement would result in
a tangent off the curved path (Figure 9).

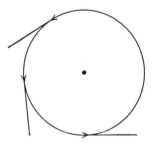

Figure 9. Note that the body direction is constantly changing in
movement through a curved path; otherwise the result would be a
tangent off the curved path.

The greatest difficulty students have with movement in a curved path is maintaining a constant relationship of the body as a whole to the axis around which they move. They often twist the upper body too far and destroy their relationship to their center by getting a front or back shoulder lead. The other basic difficulty is sensing the pull toward a central axis when the movement calls for a shifting or rotating center (see Figure 10). It takes a great deal of practice over a period of time to accomplish accuracy in movement through a curved path.

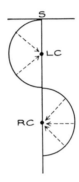

Figure 10. S: starting point; LC: left center toward which the body leans in traveling through the first curve; RC: right center toward which the body leans in traveling through the second curve. The point midway between LC and RC is where the shift is made in establishing a new center.

E. *Elevation*

The dance student spends much time and energy defying gravity. To be able to rise from the floor with ease is one of the very necessary phases of dance education. It is equally necessary to return to the floor with ease.

The most important prerequisite for efficient elevation is proper take-off and landing. This involves development of habitual good co-ordination of the whole body. Pliés, discussed earlier in this chapter, provide adequate preparation for elevation by producing the co-ordinated movement which is basic to the take-off and landing phases of elevation. In addition to proper leg alignment, body tension must be adequate to hold the body solidly in one piece. This means that the muscles of the upper back as well as the abdominal muscles and gluteals must be working in co-ordination with the extensors of the legs.

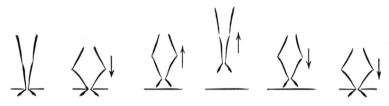

Figure 11. Elevation: take-off and landing.

Faulty elevation is not only painful to watch but also dangerous for the individual. The common faults are:

1. Arching the back on the push-off and collapsing on the landing.
2. Lacking a sense of direct vertical force.
3. Timing the take-off and landing phases poorly.
4. Bending too deeply into the floor on the landing, thus making it difficult to get off the floor again.
5. Relaxing with gravity on the landing.
6. Rebounding too slowly from the floor.
7. Dropping the knees inward on the landing.
8. Sitting into hips to break the fall.

To be able to produce beautiful elevation the student must first produce well-co-ordinated use of the body as a total unit. She must practice consistently over a period of time, concentrating on the kinesthetic awareness of the action, timing, and position throughout the elevation process.

There are many things to think about in the execution of such a highly technical feat. Controlling elevation is very much like learning to dive for the first time. It is over before one realizes what has happened. With each new attempt, one makes a correction over the last trial. After each trial, an attempt to think about what was done should be made. With constant repetition it is possible to iron out the difficulties of execution. Gradually, there is less to think about because the co-ordination becomes easier and the individual is free to concentrate on the finer points of skill.

Well-controlled elevation is executed by:

1. Maintaining a solid body which is not rigid. The student must be motivated to feel light and be ready to soar upward. This is accomplished through the lift in the chest, tightening of the upper back and abdominal muscles, and also through the attitude or frame of mind of the individual. One must feel and think upward in order to go up with ease.

2. Proper action of bending and stretching the legs in efficient timing of joint action. The student should practice feeling every part of the action muscularly, so that the fine degrees of full extension from the hips through the knees, ankles, and toes on the push-off are sensed kinesthetically. Likewise, one should reach for the floor with the toes and actively pull the body into the floor upon landing.

One may produce elevation from one place, landing in the same place, or from one place to another. Traveling elevation calls for some adjustment in body alignment. If one is traveling forward, the body must be in a position ready to move forward. However, the line of force on the push-off must be direct from the foot to the head, with no bend at the hips. The hips must be carried through space in an over-curve on top of the legs; this calls for fine control of the extensors of the hips.

Elevation is a highly technical phase of dance which must be mastered if one is to enjoy dance to the fullest. It requires control of the whole body in split-second action. However, it is challenging and fun to practice, even in the early stages of development.

F. *Dimension and suspension:*

Movement exists naturally in three principal dimensions —vertical, horizontal, and depth dimensions. It is, of course, possible to use variations of these dimensions, or to use some and exclude others if there is a purpose in such selection. However, the student should learn to use all three.

Along with the conscious use of dimension in movement, one must consider suspension. Suspension points may be in any part of the body one chooses. It is the point from which the body appears to be suspended. It is not necessarily the highest point of the movement but, rather, the plane of the body through which one feels the greatest vertical pull. Suspension points produce a stretch upward against the downward pull of gravity and give lightness to elevation and resistance to movements of downward pull.

When the student becomes aware of dimension and suspension, her movement becomes more dramatic and sensitive because she must concentrate on the sensation and motivation of such movement from within the body. Thus, a new territory for exploration is open to her. The student's movement invariably becomes more interesting. She passes from the stage of large muscle activity and total body movement to finer degrees of differentiation and shading of movement. As a result, she experiences a new sense of bodily action. In doing this she is consciously relating her movement to space. It is through conscious use of dimension that one becomes aware of the dynamics and interrelationship of movement and spatial forces.

G. *Projection:*

Projection is the technique of making contact with an audience. It is a delivery vehicle—the process of directing one's movement to an audience. Dance is performed primarily for purposes of communication. If one dances for a small audience in a small room, she addresses herself to that audience. If she dances for a large audience which is at a distance from her, she directs her movement in accordance with that distance.

Projection is the result of motivation within the dancer which causes her to give her movement vitality and direction. A dancer who is concerned solely with herself while performing rarely projects with any impact on an audience. Projection comes with maturity and is selfless in nature. The more an individual gets into her role while perfoming, the less she thinks about herself. In such circumstances she is more likely to communicate directly and convincingly.

Projection, then, is a space consciousness combined with motivation for expression and the ability to communicate one's feelings and ideas to others. It is an essential faculty for performance which is developed through well-guided dance experiences.

H. *Turns:*

Movement which pivots or turns and travels through space probably presents more technical problems than any other kind of movement.

To do an adequate job of executing turns the student must first find the central axis of the body; this is an imaginary plumb line from head to foot at the center of the body. Turning or curved movement of any kind cannot be arbitrarily controlled at will. The student must become aware of the center about which rotation occurs. Once this center is established, the individual may have some means of measuring accuracy of execution. Second, the student must learn to develop accuracy of body rotation around a shifting center while turning through space. The greatest problem is not one of finding the center but, rather, maintaining a constant relationship to that center as centrifugal and centripetal force is produced.

Turning should be taught in an even rhythm first, so that the individual learns to control her balance. Once again the common difficulty is in maintaining the body as a solid whole, avoiding a forward bend, and sitting into the hips. Students often use a step that is too large to allow for even turning, which results in poor balance. Overstepping forces students to fall into a turn that is accented and uneven. Keeping the rhythm even and the step size normal guards against a variety of idiosyncrasies and compensations for lack of balance. Each student must keep the span of her step within a range which is normal for the length of her legs.

The body weight must be carried alternately between the legs and over one leg as the weight is transferred from one leg to the other. Outward and inward rotation of the legs is necessary because turning consists of alternate outward and inward rotation in the hip joints. In plain turning, the leading leg is rotated outward on the first half of the turn and the other leg is rotated inward on the second half of the turn.

Turning is taught on a one-half basis of organization. It takes two units of a step pattern to complete a whole turn. If a walk is used, one-half of the turn is completed on the first step and the second half is completed on the second step. The same organization applies to turns using other forms of locomotion such as the skip, leap, run, gallop, and step-hop.

Spotting should be done on the first half turn or be connected with the leading foot. The individual focuses her eyes on something at the opposite end of the room in the direction of travel. As she completes the first half turn and can no longer focus there, she turns her head with the body as she completes the second half of the turn. On the second half of the turn she does not focus on anything but immediately turns the head to focus again on the first part of the next turn. In general the head turns with the body, avoiding the snap of the neck. The head is part of the turning movement and the momentary pause for spotting is hardly noticeable. Most students overcome dizziness as they become more skilled in turning. The head gets a lot of swirling in the early stages of learning, particularly when the upper back is uncontrolled. However, under proper guidance and preparation for turning, the problems of developing this skill are minimized. As in any other motor skill, practice with a goal and a means of measuring progress irons out the defects in execution.

4

Release

Activities

R ELEASE activities consist of the application of fundamental principles of movement to basic forms of locomotion.
The basic forms of locomotion are the run, walk, hop, jump,
leap, skip, and gallop. Locomotor activities present the additional problems of shifting weight and changing direction
while moving through space; they also require constant adjust-
ments for balancing. The test for the co-ordination of the body
as a total unit is the ability to maintain such control while moving through space. Such control is an absolute necessity if one
is to dance well.

Control of the body in movement through space is best
achieved by practicing locomotor activities. Release activities
provide the needed practice and at the same time yield a great
deal of satisfaction. They are truly self-testing activities. They
require the application of fundamental principles of movement, in order to be done in good form. They give the feeling
of freedom and exhilaration and require the expenditure of a
great deal of energy in a very short span of time. In this sense
they serve as tension-releasing activities that prepare the stu-

dents technically and at the same time stimulate the students emotionally.

Through release activities, the students learn to enjoy physical exertion. When students can move freely through space by directing their energy into clean and effective movement that is rhythmically organized, they are truly experiencing pleasure in movement. There is even a great deal of satisfaction to be found in the fatigue that results; the feeling of being alive, dynamic, vital, and "ready to go" is a feeling that must be stimulated and nourished.

The variations of locomotor activities included under the release activities that follow are by no means exhaustive. One could work out innumerable variations. There is no reason why release activities cannot grow naturally out of a lesson. Release activities are the result of organizing stationary movement on a locomotor base. This organization work provides a challenging problem for students. Many of the locomotor activities that arise from a class accumulate and become a favorite repertoire of locomotor activities that the students enjoy repeating the last few minutes of a class period.

Release activities are valuable in providing exciting rhythmic activities, experiences in movement variety, opportunities for sequential repetition, and practice in movement phrasing and dynamics. Above and beyond all of these values remains a very important one—release activities are fun to do.

SUGGESTED RELEASE ACTIVITIES

A. *Variations on walking:*
  1. Start with a simple walk forward and take a quick change of direction each time two accents appear in succession (music or drum). Be accurate in directional changes and utilize all directions.
  2. Improvise freely on a walking base in response to images that the teacher suggests or to moods the accompanist can set as a stimulus.
  3. Step forward on the left foot, swing the right leg for-

ward while rising to a suspension, and drop into a lunge position on the right leg. The sequence may take three or four counts, depending on the length of suspension time preferred. (If done in three counts and the tempo increased, it becomes a step-leap.)

4. Combine a double arm swing with the above exercise. Swing arms forward on the step swing and backward on the lunge.

5. Walk straight forward and work for a smooth, gliding quality. Eliminate all up and down motion. Do the same in a variety of tempos from slow to fast.

6. Take four steps forward and two backward, continuing in the same direction of travel. Pivot one-half turn on the fourth step forward and one-half turn on the second step backward. (When this is done on a running base at a fast tempo, the pivot becomes a small leap turn.)

7. Take three steps in each of the following directions, starting with the right foot: forward, left sideward, backward, right diagonal forward, left diagonal forward, right diagonal backward, left diagonal backward, right sideward, and pivot in a circle. If the above is done in unison, it is easy for individuals to see their mistakes and correct themselves. The body must be facing forward throughout the exercise. Students should work for accurate body direction.

8. Take five steps forward and three backward against a $\frac{4}{4}$ rhythm.

9. Walk forward four steps, rise on toes with hips and body straight, and hold balance for four counts.

10. Take a three-step turn on a forward right diagonal, starting with the right foot, and hold the fourth count. Do the same on the left forward diagonal. Progress through space on alternate diagonals.

11. Take two steps on a walking level and one on toes at a fast walking tempo.

12. Take a step-close-step in a forward direction; lift the

free leg forward as arms go forward; pivot one-half turn on the standing leg to face the opposite direction; pull arms out to sides and bend the leg that is lifted in back; go into a plié on the standing leg with the back arched; continue moving backward for two steps and turn to face forward on the next two steps (eight counts for total unit in ¼ time).

13. Take two vibrations to one step and progress through space, improvising with the body and arms to a syncopated jazz tune or to percussion.

14. Step forward into a small plié with arms extended sideward, the body rounded forward, and the arms crossed; straighten the body upward with arms overhead; stretch upward and lift the chest as the arms are opened to a sideward position. Use a slow tempo with two counts for each step.

15. Do plain turns with body straight and arms extended sideward. Complete each turn in two steps. Keep the rhythm even and start the turns with the side of the body facing the direction of travel.

B. *Variations on running:*

1. Run as fast and as smoothly as possible. Start with a fast run, decrease the tempo gradually, and accelerate the tempo again.

2. Run in triplets. Accent the first of every three counts by going into a small plié and taking the second and third counts on the ball of the foot. The tempo should be very fast so that one feels as though she were skimming the floor and floating through space. Carry the chest high and the arms suspended sideward or diagonally forward.

3. Turn on a base of running triplets. It takes two triplets to complete one full turn.

4. Alternate four runs, leaning forward with four bouncing runs and keeping the body almost perpendicular to the floor.

5. Alternate eight runs forward with eight runs backward, continuing in the same direction.

6. Take long runs covering the length of the room in as few steps as possible. Emphasize the reach with the forward leg, the pushoff with the back leg and the forward lean of the body.

7. Take a slow, continuous lunge and exaggerate the plié and pushoff.

8. Run in a figure eight in opposition to a partner; start at the side of the figure eight opposite your partner.

9. Run in a plié position, maintaining the body at that level without vertical movement. Swing the arms in opposition to the step.

C. *Variations on hopping:*

1. Combine one step and three hops, taking the step with a pronounced forward lean and the hops in an upright position. Carry the free leg in a bent position forward on the hops.

2. Take four step-hops in even rhythm. Alternate with the same step pattern in uneven rhythm.

3. Take a step-hop-step with as much elevation as possible and carry the free leg forward, with the arms swinging in opposition to the legs. The pattern repeats on the same side. Vary by quickly increasing the range of leg spread while the body is in the air. The split in the air must be very fast if the student is to be ready to land properly.

4. Take three runs and one hop; vary the carriage of the free leg on the hop from straight forward to bent forward or a bent position in back. The hopping leg may be straight or bent while in the air. Vary the rhythm from even to uneven, allowing a longer time for elevation.

5. Take a series of turns, using a step-hop in even rhythm. Use one step-hop for each half turn. Change the rhythm

to a skip. Alternate four even and four uneven step-
hop turns.

6. Take a series of skipping turns; make the first half turn
large and the second half turn small. Emphasize the
range of the movement by an alternate open and closed
position of the body and by an accented lift of the leg
on the first half turn.

7. Step-hop with the free leg lifted in back; on the landing, swing the free leg forward and hop again. Transfer
the weight and do the same on the other side. The
arms swing in opposition but only change when the free
leg swings forward. The pattern is as follows: step-hop-
swing-hop in ⅔ time.

8. Take a step-hop in three counts starting right; get off
the ground with a half turn in the air; land in a position facing the opposite direction; finish with two steps
backward and one step forward, pivoting on the second
step to face forward again. Repeat the sequence on the
same side.

9. Take a step-hop-hop pattern while turning and traveling across the floor. Lean toward the central axis and
lift the free leg through a high arc. Two patterns complete one turn. Extend the arms sideward to begin; on
the closing phase of the turn, bring the arms forward;
on the opening phase, raise them sideward.

10. Take five skips forward and three backward. After the
rhythm and quick change of direction are established,
do the same pattern while turning. Complete two turns
on the first four skips and take one skip in place. Reverse the movement, skipping in the opposite direction,
completing one turn with two skips and taking one
skip in place.

D. *Variations on galloping:*

1. Take a light, easy gallop straight forward, swinging both
arms forward and back; the forward arm-swing coincides

with the first gallop, and the backward arm-swing coincides with the second gallop. When the co-ordination is established, add an accent on the first gallop of every four by doubling up the legs close to the body while it is elevated. In addition, extend the body fully on the second of every four gallops. When this is well established, do the contracted position on the first and third gallops and the extended position on the second and fourth.

2. Take a gallop-leap which is diagonally directed in the body and travels in a diagonal direction through space. Start with the weight on the lead foot (right), step across with the left foot and push off for elevation with the front leg bent at the knee; keep the push-off leg straight while the body is suspended in the air; land on the forward leg. The arms swing in opposition; the left arm is forward and the right arm is sideward when the right leg is in the forward elevated position. On landing, the arms reverse to an opposition position.

3. Take a series of turns, using a gallop-leap; start with the right side in the direction of travel, with the weight on the left foot; push off from the left foot, landing on the right foot for the short step and first half turn; step left on an inward rotated leg and push from the left while rotating the body and right leg to an open, elevated position that completes the last half of the turn.

4. Take three small, fast gallops and one large, high gallop.

5. Alternate one gallop with a backward lean of the body, and one with a forward lean.

6. Take two gallops, progressing on an alternately right and left diagonal; start with the short step and do not transfer weight on the last long step of the second gallop. The pattern would be as follows: leap right, cross left, leap right, close left (do not transfer weight); leap left, cross right, leap left, close right.

7. Combine two gallops in a forward direction with two

gallops in a sideward direction. The body faces forward throughout. Repeat on the other side.

8. Take three gallops forward and one backward, bringing knees up high on the backward gallop.

E. *Variations on leaping:*

1. Do plain and even leaps first for distance, then for height, and then for height and distance.
2. Do a step-step-leap in $\frac{2}{4}$ time in a forward direction.
3. Do one leap and three steps forward in $\frac{2}{4}$ time. The rhythmic pattern would be three quick steps and one long leap, equivalent to a triplet and a quarter note.
4. Do the sequence in number three, turning. Complete the first half turn on the leap and the second half turn on the three short steps.
5. Do plain and small leap turns in even rhythm. One half turn is completed on each leap. The turns may be alternated with small leaps sideward, crossing alternately back and front, as in a grapevine step, to avoid excessive dizziness.
6. Do three runs and one leap in even rhythm. The three fast runs should build in intensity to support the leap, which should be large and forceful.
7. Do six plain leaps making three complete turns and combine with the following: leap on leading leg and go into deep knee bend; tuck the left leg under the body and lower the body to the floor on the left side; continue the circular motion by rolling from left side to right side; extend the left leg, place the foot on the floor, and resume the starting position. The sequence on the floor should be completed in six counts.
8. Organize the class in groups of threes; two of each three act as a support for the third person, who is between the other two. The third person places her hands on their shoulders and all three face the same direction. All three take three short runs; then the center student leaps

and sustains the suspended phase of the leap by supporting herself on her two partners. The student may thus analyze her mistakes more readily and sense kinesthetically the action involved in elevation.

F. *Variations on jumping:*
  1. Stand in a second position plié with arms extended sideward. Maintain the plié and travel forward by jumping without straightening the legs.
  2. Take four runs forward and two jumps in place; take off in first position, spread the legs sideward in the air, and repeat the same. The elevated phase of the jump may be varied as follows:
     a. The legs may be spread forward and back with both knees bent.
     b. The knees may be bent to opposite sides with feet together.
     c. The legs may be spread with one forward and straight and the other backward and bent.
     d. One leg may be bent sideward and the other straight sideward in opposite directions.
     e. Both legs may be bent and pulled up forward or backward in an arched position or sideward in a lateral bend position.
  3. Stand in an upright position with arms extended forward from the shoulders. Contract the body, bend the arms, and take a small plié as preparation for jumping. Push off with the feet and extend the body and arms straight upward; land on one foot and run three more steps; repeat. The rise from the floor should be percussive, and the running should be smooth.
  4. Do the following sequence in a moderate tempo with rhythmic accuracy ($\frac{4}{4}$); run, run, jump; hop, hop, jump; skip, skip, jump; gallop, gallop, jump.
  5. Take four runs and one jump, varying the leg position in the air; land on one leg and go into a deep sitting bow

and rise. The jump, elevation, sitting bow, and rise should be executed in eight counts, making the total a twelve count phrase.

SUMMARY

Body conditioning, fundamental movement experiences, and release activities are grouped together because they comprise the foundation for further development in dance. They are all important facets of the total picture of dance education. In the early stages of development, not only are these three phases of movement experience of equal importance, but also each is an integral part of the others, as shown in the lessons on fundamental movement experience.

It is particularly important in the early stages of development that students get a broad view of dance with a balance of physical skill and creative activity; such a perspective not only will provide a more secure foundation for further development, but also will shape their future viewpoints and attitudes toward dance.

The conditioning exercises as a unit are not placed first because they should be done first, nor are the release activities placed last because they should be done last. Only the sections on fundamental movement experience exist in a form that makes them readily usable as lessons. They exemplify the teaching method that makes functional use of the material included as conditioning and release activities. The conditioning exercises are grouped together and organized from the standpoint of their inherent values. This makes the materials more usable in planning lessons. The same is true of the release activities. The "fundamental" in the problems presented in "Fundamental Movement Experiences" is that of "processing" the movement that arises in conditioning activities and developing that movement into an expressive and communicative form. The form of development taken by such movement extends itself into release activities.

The organization of materials in this book does not necessarily represent sequence of experiences that will be most beneficial to all dance classes. However, from the materials given, the teacher should be able to select and develop a plan to suit the needs of her classes at their particular levels of development.

5

Improvisation

T RUE improvisation is the act of composing on the spur of the moment. This necessarily means that there is no planning involved, and, therefore, spontaneity is at its highest during such activity. The individual who is improvising must use some stimulus to awake in herself a response.

In order to develop skill in such a situation, the individual must discipline her thinking and be able to concentrate so thoroughly on the stimulus that she loses herself in the activity.

Music is often used as a stimulus for the beginner because she is familiar with it and has experienced enough of it to have many associated feeling states upon hearing it. However, there are many other types of stimuli which serve the purpose just as adequately as music. If music is used, the beginner must be given something definite on which to base her improvisation. Some students respond more strongly to rhythm, some to melody, some to mood, some to ideas that are aroused by music, and others respond to a combination of these.

Improvisation will be most successful if the teacher knows her group and starts where their interests lie, regardless of whether or not she considers their taste particularly good. (However, it is not necessary to rely on the latest hit tunes to capture their interests.) The best results are obtained by teach-

94

ers who believe in the principle of improvisation, who do not have any qualms about improvising themselves, and who are not embarrassed to improvise for the students, if necessary, in order to convince them that it is not impossible. She should encourage the efforts of students who have feelings of inadequacy.

Getting a group started on improvisation is sometimes difficult. It is necessary to have the foundation laid for improvisation through an exploration of movement during class lessons, such as the development outlined in Chapter 3. If the creative experience is gradually developed from simple to increasingly difficult problems, improvisation becomes a natural part of the continuum of creative development. Thus, the student who has inhibitions will more readily take part in solving her problems if she is gradually initiated into improvisation. The student is embarrassed when she worries about how she looks and what others think of her. She considers herself the focus of attention and doesn't realize that she is just one of a group. Self-consciousness blocks the effort of such individuals. Most high school and college students have inhibitions to varying degrees; but when they are made aware of the fact that intensive concentration will remove inhibitions, they usually work hard to gain the necessary control in disciplining their thoughts. By concentrating on the stimulus and movement, they lose consciousness of themselves.

In the beginning stages, improvisation is more successful when it is presented in the form of an exploratory problem on which the whole class works individually but simultaneously. The student should move as she feels in response to a stimulus. She should practice becoming aware of what she has just done rather than what she *might* do while improvising. She should know when a movement feels "right." She should also search for variety in movement.

Group improvisation necessarily should follow individual improvisation, since its success depends partly on the variety of movement and spontaneity of the individuals in the group.

In group improvisation, the individual strives to create movement which is dynamically related to other members of the group. At this stage of development it is impossible to reconstruct such movement, but it is possible to be aware of the related group movement. It is also a good plan to have sections of the class watch other, more practiced groups and see movement that is spontaneously organized and "right."

It is very simple to tell when one is *planning* movement during improvisation, particularly in group improvisation. In such cases the responses or reactions to the movement of others are timed poorly; students work too hard at contrasting their movement to others, or they copy movement of others rather unconvincingly. Spontaneity is lacking. The face usually shows concentration on what someone else is doing. Spontaneity is the essence of vitality, the quality that keeps a dance alive and the principle upon which "right now" learners are developed. "Right now" learners are students who actively grasp what is being taught at the time it is presented. They organize information and apply it to themselves immediately. They are vitally interested in the activity and are ready to contribute their ideas without hesitation. They are living the things they do rather than thinking about doing them. Spontaneity is a personality characteristic which the great majority of students can possess if they are willing to work for it. It can be acquired through creative activity.

Improvisation serves as a basis for finding appropriate movement to express ideas and feelings one may wish to use for a dance. To have a wealth of improvisation experience is to have an extensive source from which to draw movement ideas. When one develops skill in improvisation, she can use any type of stimulus as a means of getting and formulating dance content. Her response to the content will become organically related to her experiences in such a situation. Improvisation is the means through which the student will construct emotional line, re-experience the essence of the idea to be expressed, and find the organic form of the dance.

Before beginning the study of improvisation, the student should have experienced some discovery and exploration of movement on different levels and in different qualities of movement. She should be well acquainted with rhythm and movement dynamics. She should enjoy moving freely and be ready to study improvisation in an intensive manner.

Before going into the study of improvisation intensively, which is necessary for the development of the skill needed in

order to master it, it is best to discuss what improvisation means to the group. In the early stages, considerable encouragement and analysis is necessary in order to reach a point of progress where the student is ready to deal more deeply with improvisation.

Inhibition disappears rapidly if an experimental and permissive climate is maintained in class. The sooner one can foster the idea that the group as a whole is sharing a common problem and working for a common goal, the sooner one gets spontaneous criticism from the students. Students begin to analyse each other's successes and failures and relate them to themselves. They learn a great deal from each other when they arrive at the point of seeing movement relationships of groups.

The following problems in improvisation are designed to get response in movement to a variety of different stimuli. There are many possibilities which are not covered in this section. Anything which serves as a stimulus arousing a response may be used for improvisation problems. Additional suggestions are listed following the specific problems.

IMPROVISATION PROBLEM I

　　A. *Organization:* Individual, with the whole group active at once.

　　B. *Stimulus:* Music.

　　C. *Procedure:*

　　　　1. Make a selection of several pieces of music, either piano pieces or recordings. The music should vary in its strong points. For example, one piece should have a definite mood, another should be high in its idea-association value, another should be rhythmic. One might choose a folksong, a heavy or dramatic piece, a blues, something light, and a strongly syncopated jazz tune. It is very important to select music which the group will respond to regardless of their taste in music.

　　　　2. Have the group move as the music makes them feel. They should be aware of the fact that every piece of

music is not necessarily going to stimulate them, and that all the movement they make is not going to feel right to everyone. However, it is best for them to keep moving, for they learn a great deal when they realize their way of moving may not be an appropriate or acceptable response to the stimulus.

a. The student should not allow herself to repeat a few movements over and over; rather, she should search for new ways of moving.

    b. It is sometimes necessary to discuss the process of finding different ways of moving, such as finding a movement that one feels interesting and then trying to do it with another part of the body. The same movement may be done on a variety of different levels, may vary in size from very small to very large, and may be done with locomotion.

  3. Ask for descriptive terms for what the group felt as a response to the stimulus. Some students respond predominantly to melody, others respond more to rhythm, and some to quality of instruments. A few students are able to develop complete situations after only one hearing. The group may then choose one piece on which they would like to concentrate. They may improvise to the same piece and develop more definite ideas on which to base their movement. It is often good to let a group improvise several times to the same music if there is a particular piece that is interesting to them. True, they are doing a certain amount of planning of movement in all their attempts after the original response, but this has value too, as will be evidenced later in the discussion of composition.

IMPROVISATION PROBLEM II

  A. *Organization:* Groups of six to eight students.

  B. *Stimuli:* Movement and music.

  C. *Procedure:* In group improvisation the individual is responding both to the music and to the movement of others in the group. The music serves as a common stimulus to the whole group.

    1. Within groups, have everyone move to the stimulus (music) first, and limit the area so they are required to hold together as a group.

    2. Using the same stimulus, have them consciously try to move together and react at every opportunity when they are stimulated by other members of the group.

3. The individuals improvising should attempt to recognize moments when they are so related to the movements of others that they feel an immediate sense of organized motion taking place.

D. After group reactions have begun to appear, alternate the

groups, allowing one group to watch another so that they get a visual as well as kinesthetic impression of those well-organized moments for which they strive through improvisation. When they are able to see movement responses which are dynamically related, well timed, and spontaneous, they have a clear picture of what they are striving for.

IMPROVISATION PROBLEM III

A. *Organization:* Couples, with all couples active at once.
B. *Stimuli:* Design and form.
C. *Procedure:*

1. Have the couples line up across the back of the defined working area with one member of each couple on each side of center.
2. Have couple one lead out forward, two following, then three, etc. The couples may start at any time and go in any direction they desire.
3. Each person must mirror the movement of her partner and must maintain a symmetrical design in relation to the dividing line between right and left halves of the working area.
4. Partners should move together by mutual agreement. One is bound to lead part of the time and follow part of the time. Movement should be slow enough to allow changes to happen naturally instead of being forced. Students should relate their movement to other couples by moving into a position of contrast to those they are near at any given time. They do this by sensing motion around them rather than by watching others. They may travel any place within the defined area.
5. If music is used, it should be slow enough to allow partners to keep together. A drum beat or rhythms on percussion instruments may be used to establish some rhythmic organization.

IMPROVISATION PROBLEM IV
  A. *Organization:* Individual.
  B. *Stimulus:* Drumming or recorded drumming (rhythm).
  C. *Procedure:*
      1. Play a steady and even drum beat of eighth notes. Tempo should be moderately fast. An excellent drumming record, called "Drums of Haiti," 403, LP, is recorded by Ethnological Folkways Library.
      2. Have the group do a small bounce up and down, letting the knees bend but feeling the body move as a total unit; they should keep their heels on the floor and the pulse even and constant.
      3. After the bounce is established, break out of the constant pulse with accented movements and return to the vibration, again keeping the movement rhythmically accurate. The pulse must be maintained somewhere in the body when one breaks away from the bouncing movement. All accent or pause should be related to the underlying beat.
      4. The tempo of this problem causes the individual to move in a percussive manner and requires her to concentrate on the rhythm. Consequently, her movement is usually more spontaneous, forceful, and primitive in style.
      5. While using the bounce and pulse, alternate stop action with it; do eight bounces and strike a new position on the accent of one; follow through with sustained movement for the remaining seven counts, keeping the pulse alive; then come back to the bounce again and repeat.
      6. Take four bounces in place followed by explosive movement twice as fast as the bounce; accent each beat. Explosive movement should be sharp, clean, and quick. Keep repeating the sequence until the students are able to move fast enough to be accurate.
      7. Organize groups of three or four and have them im-

provise together to the drumming within the problem as it is set.

IMPROVISATION PROBLEM V

A. *Organization:* Small groups of six to eight people.
B. *Stimulus:* Movement.
C. *Procedure:*

1. Place individuals of each group at random around the edge of the working area.
2. Have one person start a movement theme. As she moves in the direction of another person, that person picks up the theme which the first person has set; the first person then moves toward another, thus setting up a chain reaction. All individuals are then improvising in relation to each other on the theme set at the beginning.
3. Encourage interchange of small groups so that individuals do not remain with the same group. With eight people there are many possibilities in groupings of 2-2-4; 1-3-4; 2-3-3; etc.

IMPROVISATION PROBLEM VI

A. *Organization:* Groups of eight to eleven students.
B. *Stimuli:* Form and music.
C. *Procedure:*

1. Teach the class a set phrase of movement in 16 counts to be done in unison. This can be as simple as marching in a stylized manner 4 steps forward, 4 steps backward, 6 steps in a circle of their own, jump on 7, and hold count 8. Practice until they can execute the phrase in unison.
2. Place each person in a definite position and the group in a definite place. Execute the 16 count phrase in unison. Improvise the next 16 counts, moving away from that area but arriving back in time to come in on the unison phrase.
3. The improvised section may be of another quality or

mood and may change rhythmically, but the phrase length should be the same. If one has an accompanist, the improvised section can be of a different quality each time it appears. If one uses percussion, the rhythm and choice of instruments can be changed for the improvised section.

IMPROVISATION PROBLEM VII
  A. *Organization:* Individual.
  B. *Stimulus:* Mood extracted from either music or a situation.
  C. *Procedure:*
    1. Choose a piece of music which strongly expresses a particular mood, or work out a dramatic situation through which the student may experience a particular mood.
    2. Let the group improvise to either or both of these stimuli. When they finish, have them describe their experiences in writing in an attempt to define the mood for themselves.
    3. Let them discuss the feelings they had while moving. Draw out their ideas and clarify them so that everyone has an understanding of what constitutes a mood.
    4. Have them improvise on the mood they have extracted. Have them set a theme or phrase which they feel expresses the mood.
    5. Let them improvise on this theme.
    6. Let them discuss the differences found in working with and without music.
    7. Have the class evaluate the results and point out the reasons why the successful themes were successful in expressing the intended mood.

IMPROVISATION PROBLEM VIII
  A. *Organization:* Couples.
  B. *Stimulus:* Movement.

C. *Procedure:*

1. One person of each couple executes a movement phrase or statement in the form of a question. The other partner responds immediately as an answer to the movement of the first person.

2. Work with phrases of increasing length and give everyone a chance to set the question and respond with an answer.

   a. If the person who sets the question has a definite idea in mind, the movement is more likely to evoke a response.

   b. The person responding must be open to stimulation and ready to react.

3. When two people have sufficient experience and are able to respond easily, keep the conversation in movement going with each person alternately responding to the other until the development of an idea or situation appears.

4. Have each couple try to reconstruct something they improvised in response to their partner and set it so they can remember the movement in its natural rhythmic organization. Development of the ability to remember improvisation is difficult but necessary.

IMPROVISATION PROBLEM IX

A. *Organization:* Couples.

B. *Stimuli:* Situations.

C. *Procedure:* Present the following situations.

1. Two individuals meet on the street, recognize each other in some way, and resolve their reactions. Each person should imagine the person she is meeting as a particular person she has known, so that there is some motivation for her reaction.

2. The instructor can set such a situation and define the two characters to insure a definite reaction. For example:

a. You are meeting an old cherished friend whom you haven't seen for five years.

b. You are meeting a person who is familiar but whom you are not sure you have met. You are uncertain whether or not you should recognize her.

c. You see a person ahead of you whom you recognize as an old friend. You hurry to catch up to him or her, give a raucous old greeting with a slap on the

back. When the person turns around, it is not the person you thought it was; it's a perfect stranger.

3. Discuss the responses, indicating general faults. If the responses are in the form of pantomime, have them abstract the pantomime, keeping the essence of the response the same (see p. 122, Problem 1, for abstraction).

4. Have the more interesting results demonstrated and point out the similarities and differences among them.

5. Discuss the principle of spontaneity and the problems involved in reconstructing a spontaneous situation or reaction.

IMPROVISATION PROBLEM X

A. *Organization:* Groups of ten to twelve students.

B. *Stimulus:* Words.

C. *Procedure:*

1. Choose a number of isolated words, such as "who," "how," "oh," "come," "leave," etc.

2. The instructor says a word with a particular inflection which will imply meaning. It may be a command, a question, a sympathetic response, or begging. The word is given and the group reacts in response to their own interpretation.

3. After using a combination of several words which may be used many times with different inflections, question the students for their interpretations. For example, "who":

  a. May be used with an inflection which suggests a sympathetic feeling, as though one were saying, "Who are these poor people?"

  b. May be used to command an explanation for a misdemeanor. "Who left this bicycle for me to trip over?"

  c. May be used as a question to repeat something not quite heard. "Who is it?"

4. Develop a situation spontaneously by letting the group response serve as a stimulus to the teacher. Thus, her words will be a response to the group reaction. A chain of responses will take place between the leader and group, with one responding in movement and the other in words.

IMPROVISATION PROBLEM XI

A. *Organization:* Various-sized groups, depending on individual problems.
B. *Stimuli:* Ideas and situations.
C. *Procedure:*
  1. Have ideas or situations which offer opportunity for movement responses typed on index cards (see page 113).
  2. Call on the appropriate number of people to execute the idea and give them the card. When they have read the information, have them start improvising immediately. The accompanist should also have the idea, since she will be improvising with them. However, an accompanist is not essential.
  3. Have the group of observers state what they understand the improvisation to be. Question how they got their interpretations and what cues led them to interpret the way they did.
  4. Following the above discussion, read the idea to them so that they can see what was intended.
  5. Discuss the success or failure of the improvisation, with concrete examples from the improvisation itself.
  6. Following are examples of such ideas and situations. One of the simplest ways of getting ideas or situations of interest is to have the students write down an experience they have had which was unusual or interesting. Take these ideas and restate them so that they are clear and simple to understand. For example:
  a. It is a cool summer evening in the mountains. You

are startled by the cry of a wild animal. You summon someone out of bed to investigate, and nothing can be found. After settling down, the cry is heard again and very close to the house. You summon the individual out of bed again and you cannot decide whether or not to brave the outside. Resolve the situation.

b. You are going through a large cavern 2,000 feet underground. It is damp, silent, and dark. Show how you would feel in this situation.

c. You are walking up Broadway in New York City with a friend from a foreign country. This is her first trip to a metropolitan area. She becomes absorbed in something and gets left behind in the crowd. When you suddenly realize you have lost her, you make a mad search for her among the crowd.

d. You are running alongside a city bus, trying to get it to stop for you. It finally stops at the next red light. You catch up with it, only to find it is the wrong bus.

e. You are making a practice sprint in cross-country running and become very tired. Some other people with more zip than you come whizzing by so fast that you are literally blown out of their way. It is easier to sit than to stand, so you sit down. Just as you think you cannot move under any circumstances, you look beside you and see a rattlesnake approaching. Resolve the situation.

f. You are alone in a strange city when a man walks alongside you. He is persistent, stares at you, stops when you stop, walks when you walk. Your problem is to get rid of him.

g. You are very ill at ease playing the piano for the first time in public. You shake with stage fright as you go on stage. You get through the ordeal with some difficulty and are still ill at ease when you finish—even though the audience has clapped.

h. You are being initiated into a club and are required to steal some articles from the ten cent store. Having a great deal of fear about stealing, you go through with the assignment and take your wares back to the club. You are then told that it was all arranged with the store to let you get away with it.

i. You are trying to make your first dive off a diving board. Your big problem is getting enough nerve to do it. Finally, you do it, not because you have the nerve, but because you are off balance when you got to the end of the board.

j. You are in a dream; your knees are made of rubber and bend in odd directions. They just don't work as you think they should and you struggle to figure out why you find yourself in such odd positions.

k. You are at a very polite and proper party trying to impress someone when you suddenly feel your slip working its way down. You try to ignore it, but it gets the best of you. You excuse yourself and move toward the powder room. The slip gives way and drops completely to the floor.

l. You are giving an after-dinner speech.

IMPROVISATION PROBLEM XII

A. *Organization:* Individual.

B. *Stimuli:* Auditory, visual, and tactile stimuli and associations with objects.

C. *Procedure:*

1. Have the students do spontaneous, improvised compositions as a response to any of the following stimuli. They must start moving immediately after the stimulus is given.

2. It is best to have the students close their eyes when experiencing either auditory or tactile stimuli.

a. *Auditory:* door bells, phone, siren, scratching nails on blackboard, dog barking, alarm clock, splashing of water, breaking glass, pulling a cork out of a bottle, etc.

b. *Tactile:* feeling a piece of fur, wire, sand paper, fleecy wool, velvet, silk, something ice cold, money, marble, a piece of wood with jagged edges, etc.

c. *Visual:* seeing a grotesque mask, a piece of sculpture, a book, a picture of a situation which makes a strong statement, a painting, handcuffs, an evening gown, an orchestral instrument, a handsome man, or a beautiful woman.

d. *Props:* using props such as the following in the movement response: a rope, Gay Nineties bathing suit, chair, megaphone, bouquet of flowers, candle and holder, drum, book, bath towel, stole, bucket, etc. It should be possible to handle the prop without too much difficulty during movement.

The improvisation problems are not arranged in a set order that is to be followed. The teacher should select and adapt the problems that will answer the needs of her group at different levels of development. With beginning students who have no skill in improvisation, it is better to have the whole class improvise on an individual basis and then go into smaller group improvisation as soon as possible. Beginners are generally able to do better group improvisation if they have developed motor imagery through individual work. Individual improvisation offers them an opportunity to develop their own style and movement ideas. With this experience they will be more valuable group members.

The natural progression in developing this skill follows the creative plan. The students begin to improvise by just moving, with no specific idea. In the early stages it is a case of movement for movement's sake. As students gain experience they become aware of meaningful associations while moving. They try to remember these fleeting experiences in order to set them. After analyzing particular associations aroused by the movement, they can use these movements in the expression of ideas. At this point they have arrived at the stage of development where they are ready to study composition more intensively.

The particular stimulus one uses is very important if the movement experience is to be a successful one. It is one thing to use an ambiguous stimulus and another to use a stimulus that leaves no impression on the student. One cannot honestly respond to something which does not stimulate her. For example, the value of having a group respond to colors by calling out "green," "purple," and so on is questionable, as are some of the non-objective paintings that have been used. How honest a response can one get from a painting that is not understood? It is not enough to get movement—one should be looking for meaningful movement that has its roots firmly planted in reality. If the average high school or college student is left with a vague impression upon hearing or viewing stimuli, her response will show it. Most often such movement response bears no relationship to the stimulus and might be quite typical of the response one would get to any stimulus that did not really impress the student. One should not be satisfied with vague results, but should work for legitimate, spontaneous, organically related, and meaningful response in improvisation.

Improvisation is a means of producing the essential elements for dance composition. The intensive study of improvisation results in the development of a broad movement background in a relatively short period of time. Improvisation is spontaneity training. It is also a method of getting the feel of movement dynamics and of developing a more sound organic response to various kinds of stimuli. The development of these skills leads directly to reduction in the amount of time needed to compose dances and provides the student with resources for composing.

The most direct method of finding or creating movement to express an idea or feeling is by responding to that idea or feel-

ing in movement. The intellectual phase comes in as a disci-
plinary measure in evaluating or readjusting the essential
movements after they are created. The more one moves with
kinesthetic awareness, the richer her background of movement
experience will be. Such a background provides a means to
pleasurable experience in dance composition. The student with
extensive experience in improvisation has many facilities at her
finger tips for solving composition problems. These problems
can become very time-consuming if students are not adequately
prepared to handle them.

Although the emphasis here is on the positive side for improvisation as a prerequisite for good composition, such results
are not impossible without improvisation training. Regardless
of whether or not students have adequate training in improvisation, they must still go through the exploratory steps in finding
appropriate movement. If such exploration is trial and error,
they are, in a sense, practicing improvisation. If they plan their
movement unit by unit, the process becomes very tedious and
time-consuming. Improvisation is not a "must" for composition, it is an asset whch makes composing more pleasurable and
less time-consuming.

6

Dance

Composition

When one composes a dance she must create movement which expresses her idea. The movement must be organized into a form which has unity, rhythm, and spatial organization.

There are many elements of composition used in dance to make movement more expressive, such as the use of variety, contrast, dynamics, design, dramatic line, and rhythmic variation. To say that a finished composition should embrace all elements would be placing limitations or requirements on dance which should not exist. It would provide a convenient classification and serve as a quick check list for evaluation, but it would also regiment the creative process. Very few things in life are absolute; the great majority are relative. Dance composition, which uses life as its subject matter, is also a relative matter. The student creates out of her experiences. These experiences vary greatly from one individual to another and are relative to a person's background and environment. Her particular way of expressing an idea will be quite different from another person's way of expressing the same idea.

There is no end to the variety of studies one can use for practice in composing dances. It is better to start with short studies, for the student can then learn principles of composition in a shorter time and gain a broader background of experience by doing a variety of studies. It is also better to compose in small groups, using three to five students in the early attempts. This eliminates the confusion that would result from receiving too many suggestions at once. It also avoids getting involved in moving numbers of people and losing sight of the objective. Through group composition each student benefits from the ideas of the others and also acts as a critic for the others.

The early group composition experience should be a real group effort. This means that all individuals in the group should be responsible for the development of the project and all should contribute directly through movement ideas and suggestions. In composing a dance it is necessary to have a group leader who makes good use of the suggestions of group members. It is also necessary to define clearly the function of this group leader, whose job is one of organizing the group and steering progress so that everyone works in an effort to contribute something to the composition.

The following composition problems were selected for beginning students. They do not represent all types of problems or the ultimate in composition. They are not arranged according to any set order for use. Whether one starts with pantomime or with ideas that are less concrete is dependent entirely upon what the group is ready for. The students who have developed skill in improvisation are likely to have many ideas on how to find the right movements to solve a problem, and they would be ready to work with more intangible problems such as moods, character studies, or movement themes. On the other hand, many students prefer having something concrete in their first attempts. They would be more comfortable with a type of problem which uses gesture or pantomime as its basis.

The problems suggested here are varied. Form problems and movement problems should have motivation. For that matter, all movement should be motivated. This does not mean that one must explain the meaning of her movement verbally. But it does mean that movement should be created from some motivation if it is to communicate something. For example, a group may decide to do a movement study. If they so desire, they should base their study on a movement problem such as dynamics and space relationships, quality and style, or a particular attitude or mood. In such a study they should develop a definite attitude or quality, and the problem of interrelationship of movement dynamics and space must reflect this. They do not simply decide to do a movement problem and pull it out of nowhere. Their movement should be motivated, and the result of the study should have some communication value in terms of a feeling of excitement, a pleasing quality, or kinesthetic pleasure in experiencing the movement. The dance composition should communicate some sense of feeling to the spectator. It should be a kinesthetic and emotional experience that may be intellectualized later.

Studies in composition should never be accepted (as they sometimes are) with a "that's nice" attitude. If the results are good, the reasons for that opinion should be pointed out. If the study falls short of the goal, the results should be analyzed and suggestions for improvement should be offered. A great deal of learning takes place when a group of students become aware of their responsibility to make suggestions and criticize the dances of the other class members. It is a good plan to throw out leading questions to the group, after they have viewed a study, in an attempt to lead their discussion into an analysis of what has been done. An instructor should never accept student comments such as "It was terrific" or "Wonderful," without probing for the reasons for their reactions. The teacher has a golden opportunity to help students analyze why they like or dislike what they see. It is needless to say that all criticism should be constructive. If the teacher and students point out shortcomings, they should follow up with concrete suggestions on how the studies can be improved.

Student creative effort is often not put to the test of criticism and reworking. Students are often led to believe that whatever they do is good because it is their own. One of the best ways of raising standards of student creative effort is to give constructive and concrete criticism which will make them want to improve and rework their composiitons to achieve clarity and artistic expression of their ideas. It is equally important to emphasize the strong as well as the weak points of students' compositions so that they experience satisfaction with the progress they have made and at the same time recognize that there is room for improvement.

PROBLEM I: Abstraction of Gesture and Pantomime
  A. *Explanation:*
    1. Gesture is a movement which carries specific meaning, as exemplified in thumbing a ride, beckoning someone to come, holding the head when one has a headache, waving goodbye, etc.
    2. Pantomime refers to acting out realistically a situation or activity such as getting out of bed, playing the violin, washing dishes, taking a shower, etc.
    3. Abstraction means changing or varying a gesture or movement from its natural form so that it becomes more highly suggestive and less definitive. Abstraction is a process of variation; the essential characteristics of the gesture or situation must be maintained regardless of the degree of abstraction an individual prefers to use.
  B. *Procedure:*
    1. Divide the class into small groups. Let them choose any gesture they would like to work with. If each group chooses a different gesture, the class will benefit by seeing how different groups solve their particular problems and how differently each gesture may be treated.
    2. Pantomime or gesture is abstracted by the following methods:
      a. Changing the rhythmic organization from its natu-

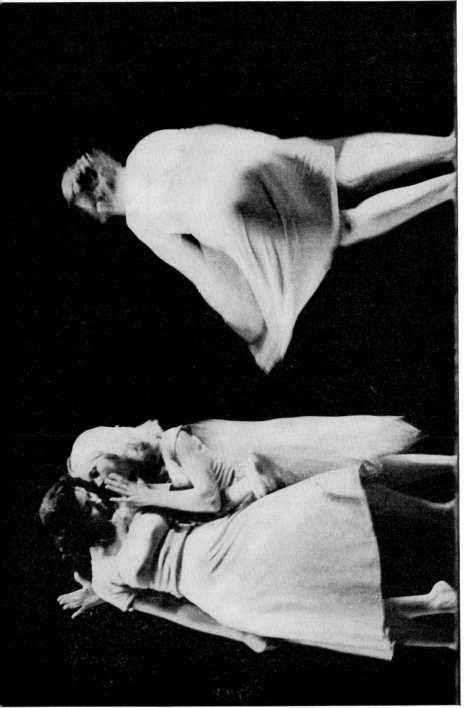

ral form (by varying the rhythmic pattern, tempo, and accent).

b. Increasing or decreasing the amount of tension needed to perform the movement.

c. Varying the range of the movement from very large to very small.

d. Changing the direction of the movement.

e. Adding movement in other parts of the body to support the movement.

f. Transferring the movement to another part of the body.

g. Varying more than one element of the movement at once by combining two or more of the variations simultaneously.

h. The above results may be executed by a group in forms such as unison, antiphonal, and successional, or two gestures may be combined for an ABA form.

C. *Students should experience:*

1. A broader perspective on how infinite movement varition is.

2. Practice in taking one idea and developing it through restatement in a number of different ways.

3. Discovery of the limits of abstraction (degree of abstraction where the movement becomes vague or lacking reference to the original movement).

4. Practice in building a dance composition from a small amount of material.

5. Practice in organizing movement into a form suitable for a group.

PROBLEM II: Focus

A. *Explanation:*

1. Focus is concentrated projection of the body in a particular direction. It establishes a center of interest between the person moving and an object or between

the person and space, or it establishes the person in relation to another individual or group.

2. Focus is not necessarily associated with the direction in which a person is looking. Actually, the head is only part of the total picture. The body may establish the focal point of interest with the head turned in another direction. The back of the head also may be used in establishing focal interest.

B. *Procedure:*

1. Studies in focus should be used with content. The group may experiment with focus through improvisation, discover an idea through this process, and then utilize this form in expressing the idea.

2. The instructor may set the idea for the problem by

   a. Designating a particular spot in the working area toward which all movement must be focused. It may be presented as a situation for improvisation first and constructed into a composition later. For example, a crowd is milling about aimlessly, and gradually individuals begin to discover something on top of a tall building. At random, they gather into one group, following suit to see what the others see until the whole group focuses their movement to one specific focal point. It is an interesting experiment to have a nucleus group of two or three people move out of the crowd and establish the focal interest. The rest of the group should not be informed of what the others are doing. The group as a whole would be instructed to be a crowd, milling about and ready to react to anyone or anything they might see. Eventually, the group would arrive at a concentrated focal point.

   b. Setting a situation where all individuals are attracted to one area. Some may desire to go there, some may resist it. (Example: the scene of an accident.)

    c. Giving the group the freedom of moving any place but always maintaining the focus of the head toward one particular place. It is generally better to let the individual supply her own imaginary object toward which she directs her movement.

C. *Students should experience:*

1. The discovery of how one projects bodily movement toward a definite focal point.
2. Realization that focus involves the whole body, which is projected toward a particular place.
3. The development of ideas suitable for expression through this particular spatial form.
4. Practice in composing with dramatic content.
5. A kinesthetic awareness of the tractive force between the focal point and the body.
6. An awareness of texture in space.

PROBLEM III: Mechanics of Group Composition

A. *Explanation:* Learning to do group composition is not difficult provided the students know how to go about it. Group composition means a project produced by a group. This type of composition can be illustrated by handling the whole group at once.

B. *Procedure:*

1. Choose someone out of the group to come to the front and set four measures of movement. Have the whole group learn it. Choose another to do the same, continuing on from the first four measures but contrasting her movement to the first four measures. Have the group learn that also, so the total eight measures can be performed with ease. Repeat the process with another person. If the movement phrase ends with the third person, take it as a complete unit. If it doesn't end, have a fourth person do four measures which will bring the phrase to a conclusion.

2. Organize the class into divisions of small groups such as a group of twelve divided into three parts—4, 5, 3. If the class is large, organize several such groups so that several compositions will be going at once.

3. Place the groups in a particular arrangement within their designated working area and experiment with different forms and methods of moving groups while using the movement theme which all of the students know. Draw from the students suggestions for moving the groups and try their ideas. If their ideas work out satisfactorily, use them and ask for further suggestions. If their suggestions do not work, the students will have the experience of realizing why they do not work, and they can alter their ideas until they find a suitable form for the movement.

4. Continue this process until the form is interesting and the study has a beginning, middle, and end.

5. Following are suggestions for manipulating groups:
   a. Have each of the units of the group (that is, the smaller groups of 4-5-3 within each twelve) do a phrase of 16 measures by having the second unit (5) start the whole phrase four measures later than the first unit(4); the third unit(3) might start four measures after a second unit, establishing a canon effect.
   b. Have one unit of the group do the whole phrase while you vary the order of the phrase with the other two units.
   c. Have groups interchange at various places in the phrase.
   d. Have the whole group do the phrase in unison, followed by the first four measures; then repeat the unison phrase, followed by the second four measures; repeat the unison phrase, followed by the third and fourth phrases of four measures.

Dramatic Study

C. *Students should experience:*
1. The development of some insight into the process of moving groups in a suitable form.
2. An understanding of how one takes a theme and develops a group study through variation of form and movement of groups.
3. Realization of the need for planning and experimentation in moving groups.
4. Realization that pooling suggestions from many people is more effective and satisfying to a group than being directed by one person.
5. A sense of personal value as a result of having contributed either directly or indirectly to the solution of the problem.
6. An understanding of the mechanics of group composition and the function of a group leader.

PROBLEM IV: Mood
A. *Explanation:* A mood is a particular frame of mind or a state of feeling. The student should strive to find the essence of a mood and express it through movement.
B. *Procedure:*
1. State the problem and let the students choose the mood which they wish to express. Suggest that it may be related to a specific experience but that the essence of the mood is the content they are striving to express and not the emotional situation itself.
2. Have each student work out a motif which expresses a mood. This may be a short phrase or a few movements. Analyze what each student has done. It is a good plan to show studies without any previous explanation to see what the group gets from them.
3. After each student has received criticism, she should rework her motif to make it more accurate in carrying the feeling she intended.
4. Take the motif and develop it through variation (see

page 122, Problem 1) into a longer study which has a beginning, middle, and end—one in which the interest builds from beginning to end. It may also be enlarged in terms of additional ideas or in relation to a specific situation. All movement used in the study should grow out of the motif.

5. Analyze the results.

6. Experiment with the effect of grouping two or three

Dilemma

different mood studies together. Start with one study and bring in two others at a logical point in the development of the first. How one combines them is dependent on the results of the individual studies.

C. *Students should experience:*

1. The process of extracting the essence of an emotional experience and expressing it in a movement form which is organically related to the experience without the use of pantomime, symbolism, or gesture.
2. The natural rhythmic organization of movement which is a direct, organic response to an emotional state.
3. The dramatic line of a feeling state.
4. An understanding of how one creates a theme and develops it.
5. Practice in setting movement in the rhythmic organization in which it naturally exists.
6. An understanding of what the essence of an emotional experience consists.

PROBLEM V: Dynamics

A. *Explanation:*

1. Dynamics pertain to force of motion. In music and movement, they have become synonomous with contrast. In dance, dynamics mean the contrast of two forces which may be physical, emotional, spatial, or sculptural; dynamics are organized either on an alternating or simultaneous plan.
2. When one does a percussive movement followed by a sustained movement, the movement is dynamic by alternate contrast. When the two contrasted movements are done at the same time, the movement is dynamic by simultaneous contrast. The effect produced by the contrasted relationship of two or more forces produces a kinesthetic thrill which is termed dynamic

3. The same principle holds true for emotional or psychological forces which may be interplayed.

4. This discussion does not assume that all contrasted movement is dynamic. The element of timing must enter in. Many movements are contrasting but lack the interplay of forces which includes organization of movement from a design and rhythmic standpoint.

B. *Procedure:*

1. Explain and demonstrate examples of dynamics in movement.

2. In groups of three to five, have the students work out a movement phrase which is dynamically interesting because it utilizes alternating and/or simultaneous dynamics.

3. Have the groups demonstrate and analyze the structure of their studies for accuracy in dynamic movement. Experiment by rearranging group members to show how one may move groups to emphasize to advantage the dynamics they have in their studies. Show how the relationship of group members plays a large part in bringing out dynamic movement.

C. *Students should experience:*

1. A kinesthetic and visual sense of dynamics in individual movement and group relationships.

2. An understanding of the many ways the body can move dynamically.

3. The realization that dynamics vitalize movement form.

PROBLEM VI: Continuous Phrase

A. *Explanation:* A dance phrase is a sequence of motion making up a choreographic pattern. The tendency in creating movement for a dance is to work out short units of movement. But it is necessary to learn to develop longer phrases which carry through the development of an idea, since they are easier for the spectator to grasp and they lend greater unity and continuity to a composition. The experience also helps break the habit of remembering a dance as a series of short segments. There should be no periods in a dance until one gets to the end.

B. *Procedure:*
1. The length of the phrase may be set in number of measures or in terms of distance.
2. There should be no limitations on type of movement, but in order to insure variation and interest in the movement the following requirements are imposed:
   a. At least three changes of direction.
   b. Two or more methods of locomotion (walk, run, hop, leap, and so forth).
   c. At least two changes of level.
   d. Two or more qualities of movement.
   e. Rhythmic variation.
   f. Curved movement and some turning.
   g. Development of interest from beginning to end.
3. The phrases should be criticized in light of the assignment.

C. *Students should experience:*
1. A sense of carrying movement through a long period of time without losing continuity.
2. A challenge in creating movement which adequately solves the problem.
3. An understanding of the function of phrasing through observation and evaluation of the results of class work.

PROBLEM VII: Space Forms

A. *Explanation:* Dance distinguishes itself from most of the other arts in being a space-time medium of expression. The use of space in dance is a very important part of the whole picture. The dancer creates an awareness of space through her movement. She does this through projection of her movement and the tensional relationships within her body. The problem here is one of setting the space form and letting the student experiment with it until she has discovered the quality of movement it suggests and has associated ideas which can be appropriately expressed through the particular space form she herself chooses.

B. *Procedure:*

1. The following space forms may be presented for experimentation:

    a. A defined area which limits the individual. It can be of any shape but should be outlined by boundaries. The student must show these limitations through her movement.

    b. Expanding space. This form is unlimited and should give the feeling that space is endless. One's movement must create the illusion.

    c. Narrow or cylindrical space. The individual is enclosed in a space in which the horizontal dimension is limited but the vertical dimension is unlimited.

    d. Depth: as though one were on a high mountain overlooking a deep canyon. The student must show the attraction of depth for long distances.

    e. Height: as though one were at the bottom of a canyon looking up.

2. Let the students make their choice of the space problem with which they would like to work. If different individuals take different problems, the group benefits by seeing how others handle the problem. As a result, they have many more ideas about the use of space than they would have if the whole class concentrated on the same problem.

3. After the group has experimented with the problems and discovered ideas which are suggested by the form of the problem, they should work their ideas within the space form and develop a study which communicates their ideas.

4. Criticize and analyze the studies.

C. *Students should experience:*
1. An understanding of the principles which govern the use of space in movement.
2. The realization that all movement is related to space but that particular kinds of content are more appropriately expressed through particular spatial forms.
3. The discovery of ideas and content for dances through

Search

experimentation with movement in definite spatial forms.

PROBLEM VIII: Character Studies

A. *Explanation:* A character study consists of a clear statement and development of the attitudes and characteristics of a specific individual or type of individual. To do a character study one must know the character she is expressing and be a keen observer of the characteristics and idiosyncrasies of that individual. She must be able to isolate personality characteristics, develop them in movement form, and organize them rhythmically.

B. *Procedure:*

1. Discuss what is meant by a character study. Have the group discuss one character in particular who is known to the group. The particular choice of character would be dependent upon the group of students.

2. Extract all the information possible about this character and show how some of these characteristics could be used to portray the individual.

3. Let the students choose a character they know. They should be sure that they select and show essential characteristics rather than imitate someone in a particular situation. The character they choose should be a definite one. Too often, students do a take-off on a few aspects of an individual when they do not have a picture of the total individual.

4. Have the students work out a theme which states the character clearly.

5. When they have their theme, they should develop it in detail, organize the movement rhythmically, set the movement, and memorize it.

6. Analyze how different individuals arrived at the studies they have. Get criticism from the group on the success of the studies in terms of how clearly the character was expressed. Question the things one knows

Character Study

about the character in each study as a result of seeing the studies.

7. Folk ballads are very useful for character studies, since most ballads are about people. If one uses folk ballads, the organization of movement into a rhythmic form is not difficult. The problem in starting with folk ballads is in getting the essentials of the character in movement without being led by the words of the song. If one uses piano music, the words are not in the way as they are in a recorded ballad. However, it is not too difficult to get good results, even with the words, if the student understands that she must show the character above and beyond the description in the words. Two excellent volumes on folk material are: Boni, Margaret and Norman Llyod, *Fireside Book of Folk Songs.* New York: Simon and Schuster, Inc., 1947. Boni, Margaret and Norman Lloyd, *Fireside Book of Favorite American Songs.* New York: Simon and Schuster, Inc., 1952.

C. *Students should experience:*

1. Practice in sifting out the predominant features of character and use these features as content in developing a dance.
2. Practice in organizing movement in a rhythmic form which is appropriate for the expression of their particular choice of character.
3. Understanding of the relationship of words and movement when they are used together.
4. More acute observation of characteristics and idiosyncrasies of people.
5. A richer understanding of the type of character they have created in their studies.

PROBLEM IX: Metric Rhythm and Movement Forms

A. *Explanation:* Rhythm functions as an organizing factor in dance when the individual relates all movement to a common underlying beat. Syncopation aids the individual in feeling rhythm and gives movement vitality. This problem uses two movement themes which the instructor has planned for the group. One theme should be composed to an even rhythm and the other to the syncopated rhythmic pattern in B1. The two themes should be contrasted in quality and the use of space.

Folk Theme

B. *Procedure:*

    1. Even theme and uneven theme:

    2. Teach the two movement themes to all students. Have the students practice until they can execute both themes without difficulty.

    3. Divide the class into groups of nine. Appoint a leader for each group.

    4. Let the students experiment with moving the groups to arrive at an interesting form for their movement themes. Following are suggestions they might try:

       a. Let part of the group do the syncopated pattern and the rest do the even pattern. Let the first part do their first measure and wait while the rest of the group do their first measure; do the same with the second, third and fourth measures, obtaining a question-answer (antiphonal) or statement-rebuttal form. They may also change the order of their measures.

       b. Have the even group do four measures, the uneven group four measures, and everyone take the syncopated pattern together.

       c. Insert the first two measures of the even pattern before the syncopated pattern and the last two measures of the even between the second and third measures of the syncopated pattern; they will be combined but alternating from one to another every two measures. Let the whole group perform this sequence. Organize it in a round or canon form, with 4 voices of two measures each. Divide the group into four parts, with each voice starting two measures apart. A space form would have to be planned in order to do the study as a round.

C. *Students should experience:*

1. Rhythmic identification with a group project.
2. A kinesthetic compulsion to move rhythmically and dynamically.
3. The relation of the rhythmic pattern to the syncopation, and the value and function of rhythm as an organizing factor in movement.
4. Insight into many ways one may move groups within a rhythmic structure and arrive at an interesting compositional form.
5. An understanding of what antiphonal and canon forms are.

PROBLEM X: Breath Rhythm Related to Expression

A. *Explanation:* Breath rhythm is rhythm which results from movement created in response to feeling states and is, therefore, generally non-metric. It is an irregular rhythmic structure and is organic in the sense that it is closely related to the feelings which motivate the movement. Therefore, any study in breath rhythm would necessarily have to take its own rhythmic structure and cannot be treated as a technical problem.

B. *Procedure:*

1. Draw out everyday experiences from the group, such as getting to school, grooming oneself, writing a letter, going shopping. Have the group act out one of their experiences, concentrating on the amount of time spent in their activity and the kind of rhythm that results.
2. Divide the group and have them show the results. Discuss the rhythmic aspect of their movement and contrast it to metric rhythm by having everyone do the same movements to a metric beat. Draw observations

from the students on what happens to movement when a rhythm is imposed arbitrarily.

3. Explain what breath rhythm is and how it functions.

4. Get suggestions of situations which have emotional involvement, such as exploring a cave, rushing to the scene of an accident, watching ski jumping or high diving, struggling to run as in a dream or to escape as in a mystery.

5. Have the students work in small groups, choosing one situation and moving in the rhythm which feels right for their situation or which builds the feeling they want to show.

6. Have the studies shown and evaluate them in light of whether or not breath rhythm resulted from a motivated situation.

C. *Students should experience:*

1. An understanding of how breath rhythm comes about.

2. An understanding of the limitations of metric rhythm.

3. The realization that all experience exists in some kind of natural rhythmic setting which is related to the specifics of the situation.

4. An understanding of the differences between metric and breath rhythm.

5. An awareness of the dynamics of rhythm as a communication factor in movement expression.

PROBLEM XI: Design

A. *Explanation:* Design is the sculptural aspect of movement which results from positional relationships of different parts of the body or postural relationships between one or more bodies. Movement design exists both in transitional movements and temporary rests in a composition. Students should be aware of design in composing, but they should avoid getting into a habit of composing by positions. (Design should not be confused with floor patterns, which are a result of movement through space.)

B. *Procedure:*

    1. Have half the class take any position that comes to their minds. Have the rest of the class look at the dominant line of the bodies and comment on the differences. Reverse the procedure so the other group can observe.

    2. Discuss the types of dominant lines and space organi-

Study in Design

zation that existed. Draw some of the varieties on the board from the positions demonstrated. The dominant line of the body generally falls into a classification of off-centered and flowing, vertical and settled, or interrupted and angular.

3. Have the class work individually to find three varieties of designs.

4. Have the class work in couples and work out three different designs relating to their partner.

5. Present the studies and have the group improve on the designs where they are not clear by suggesting position changes. Have the group watch for thematic ideas in the three designs.

6. If the couples find a thematic idea, let them work out a series of ten movements which will utilize their positional relationships and will state the theme they have in mind. If they do not have a thematic idea, let them work out a sequence of movements which change from one of their three designs to the other.

7. Have the studies presented and draw out observations from the class on what principles seem to function in movement design.

C. *Students should experience:*

1. An awareness of the design factor in movement and its function for expressive purposes.

2. An understanding of the necessity for consciously considering design as a function of dance composition.

3. An awareness of movement form through design principles.

4. Practice in relating oneself to others through movement design.

PROBLEM XII: Pure Dance

A. *Explanation:* Pure dance is a term given to dance composition which has its thematic roots and development in pure movement. Pure dance exists motorly. It does

Study in Design

not borrow or lean on any other medium of expression. Pure dance is rarely seen—it is the most mature form of movement expression and is not translatable into verbal description or sequential events. Pure dance communicates motorly and exists naturally in an abstract form. To create pure dance one must experiment motorly with the feel of movement and build meaningful movement during the experimental process. Pure dance is nonpersonal and unemotional. The movement is truly organic; that is, the essence of feeling is directly expressed in movement. Pure dance should not be confused with the usual movement problems which one assigns. Pure dance must evolve from the student or group, for it is an introspective process rather than one of applying techniques to objective movement.

B. *Procedure:*

1. Have the class take one simple movement, such as an arm swing in a standing position. Have them repeat the movement many times without accompaniment. Tell them to close their eyes and concentrate on the kinesthetic feeling of the movement.

2. After they have repeated the movement many times and feel that the movement naturally wants to go somewhere else, have them change to another movement which logically follows.

3. Select a few of the more interesting movement combinations and have them demonstrated. Point out the logic of one movement following another and the fulfillment of each movement kinesthetically. Movement which is kinesthetically conceived utilizes power, relaxation, body weight, and momentum. Kinesthetically conceived movement just happens; it is not placed, positioned, forced, or anticipated.

4. Have the class work individually again, this time searching for a sequence of movements. If the individual completely submits to this principle of work-

ing, her movement sequence will logically fall into a unified style. As she works in a concentrated way, she will find what feels right as well as find feelings in movement itself. Consequently, meaningful movement will emerge.

    5. Have the students present their sequences to the class and have the group evaluate the studies in terms of the problem that was set.

C. *Students should experience:*

    1. An introduction to composition in pure movement.

    2. A greater awareness of how movement is kinesthetically and organically conceived.

    3. Greater insight into motor imagery.

    4. Practice in introspective concentration on the nature of movement as a medium of expression.

    5. An appreciation of the need for complete freedom from idiosyncrasies and movement habits in creating pure dance.

Additional Suggestions for Composition Problems

A. Theme and variation.

B. Take one of the following characters and abstract and vary the movement: busybody, two gossips, child at play, sophisticated adult, scatterbrain, worry-wart.

C. Take a simple movement and develop it in range from the smallest to the largest possible size without changing the rhythmic pattern.

D. Resultant rhythm: the interplay of rhythm and accent of two meters. Example: one group moves to a ¾ meter for twelve counts; the second group moves to a ¼ meter for 12 counts; the third group moves on the primary accents of the two combined meters for 12 counts.

E. Ground base: A type of theme and variation in which part of the theme is apparent throughout the dance.

F. Assign an interesting rhythmic pattern to be produced in movement.

G. Do ten consecutive movements which contain no element of repetition and which are entirely unlike.

H. Set a definite spatial area and have students dramatize that space, giving it texture and content.

I. Supply objects such as a rope, chair, box, material that stretches, or others. Have the students experiment with the nature of one of these objects and try moving with the object. Develop movement which is functional with the object and develop a situation with both the movement and object being an integral part of that situation.

J. Experiment with voice sounds and use them as a stimulus for creating organic movement which expresses the same feeling as the sounds.

K. Any of the situations listed at the close of the problems on improvisation may also be used for composition. Also, ideas arising out of the improvisations are readily usable as composition problems. It is good to record such ideas as they occur and keep them for future use.

Compositions created by students fall roughly into the following classifications:

Situations: The creation of an existence of particular circumstances, places, dilemmas, and people.

Characterizations: The display of essential characteristics of a person or people. Communication of a personality through exaggeration or understatement of a person's peculiarities and characteristics.

Stylizations: The expression of feeling states through a particular recognizable style or movement idiom, such as primitive, jazz, blues, folk.

Folklore: The development of ideas and stories from folk material written or sung and communicated through movement.

Words: The use of spoken words, poetry, or prose, either as a basic idea or situation to be expressed or as an accompaniment to movement.

Symbolism: Communication through the use of objects or props of any kind that carry some representative idea. The symbol may enhance the communication either through being a functional part of the movement or as an object to which the dancers bear a particular relationship.

Dramatic: Mood or a particular emotional state communicated through movement. Such feeling may be related to a situation that motivates the movement form but is not important for the spectator to grasp.

Pure Dance: Composition which has its theme rooted in pure movement. It does not rely on dramatics, gesture or emotional line. It exists in a pure movement form.

Following is a list of titles from student compositions that may serve to acquaint the teacher with ideas. This list may also serve as a stimulus for the imagination in creating new ideas for dance compositions.

Accusation	Man's Jungle
Aftermath	Mirage
Alone	Nightmare
Argument	Nobody Understands
Conversation	On the Art of Being Bored
Created and Captured	On the Range
Date	Passive Flight
Destruction of a Haunting Image	People Are No Darned Good
Dignity	Politician
Design in Space	Prejudice
Endless Duration	Pulse
Eternal Pace	Quest
Gloomy Monday	Sacrifice
Hyprocrite	Search
I'm sorry	Soliloquy in Jazz
Intrigue	Sounds
Invitation	Study in Changing Moods
Madness	Tantrum
	Transition

Trauma for Teachers   Three Approaches to Getting
Truth Unknown   a Man
Think Not I Am as I Appear

In evaluating dance composition, the teacher should be concerned with dance form. To speak of dance form is to refer to five main structures which go into the making of a total dance. They are as follows:

Movement structure: the particular form that movement takes in terms of theme, quality, character, and dynamics; the form of movement as it is used in abstraction and variation of gesture and the motivation producing the movement; the particular relationship of movement to accompaniment.

Emotional structure: the rise and fall of emotion projected through movement; the inner feelings motivated by the images the individual has as she does particular movements. The emotional structure is a result of images and feeling states which the student re-experiences while performing a dance The emotional experience is a response to the message which she is attempting to communicate. The movement is necessarily a part of the emotional experience, since the movement is created in response to the feeling states.

Rhythmic structure: the binding factor which organizes movement into a unified whole. The rhythmic structure is the organization of time elements into a sequence which is logical for the expression of the idea. This includes tempo, phrasing, accent, rest, rhythmic pattern, and the relation of movement to the underlying beat.

Spatial structure: the dancer's relationship to forces of space. The dancer may create a particular shape and texture of space or she may create an illusion of endless space. The particular organization of space she creates is dependent on what she is attempting to communicate. The space form should be appropriate for the expression of her idea. She must define her relationship to space so that her movement will project and have direction.

Design structure: The pictorial or sculptural form of movement; the dominant pictures which remain in the spectator's visual memory after the dance has been performed. Design is the relationship of one dancer to another or the relationship of one part of the body to another part in the case of the individual dancer. The positional relationship of the dancers provides one clue to the general subject matter of the dance.

A composition should embody logical order if it is to carry the message which the dancer intends. A composition should also have a beginning, middle, and end. Movement should follow a natural course of development, with one movement growing out of another. A composition should also embody dynamics in some form, whether through rhythm, emotional factors, content, space relationships, or design.

To summarize, modern dance is the communication of one's feelings, viewpoints, or ideas through the medium of movement. Such communication is the result of assimilated knowledge of life. The dancer selects from this knowledge and choreographs through motor imagery. She fashions the content of her ideas into movement, the form of which is organically related to the original experience. She does this through a process of recalling the original feeling state or situation associated with the experience and responding to it in movement. The expression of the emotional state is then objectified, removed from the smaller, personal situation, and related to a larger frame of reference which carries universal interest.

When the student can artistically create movement to express a selected experience, and organize and develop such movement into an appropriate spatial and organic form which carries meaning and esthetic pleasure to others, she has achieved skill which demonstrates knowledge and understanding of dance as an art form.

The particular way a student expresses her feelings is dependent on her experiences. Each student may differ from others in expressing the same theme. However, there are some common denominators that all such dances have in common. This is a theory that merits further study in the form of controlled experiments. Such experiments would very likely unfold many interesting facts about dance composition, the study of which is still in a very elementary stage of development.

This particular analysis of the elements of dance composition comprises one kind of organization. There are probably as many different kinds of organizations as there are dancers. Throughout the process of development, every individual organizes and reorganizes her conceptual thinking to include these basic elements as she realizes their importance. This is as it should be, with each individual giving importance to the aspects she sees as important. These elements may exist for others under different names or forms of organization. But regardless of what one's scheme or intellectual organization might be, or what the elements are called, the larger aim remains the same. Everyone is aiming at clarity and effectiveness of communication through movement, and one approach to the conceptualizing of experience may function as well as many others.

7

Dance
Clubs

Dance clubs are organized for the purpose of providing additional experience for students who desire it. The dance club provides an opportunity for students to pursue a specialized interest beyond what is offered in dance courses. In most schools the dance club is a performing group—and rightly so, since dance is a performing art. The dance club provides opportunities for students to create dances which express their own ideas and to present artistic works which they have created. Dance clubs are a means of constructively channeling student energy and effort. The dance club also provides opportunities for working closely with groups of people who share similar interests. The personal growth gained by the student through creative group work is an integral part of her total education.

ORGANIZATION

The dance club is most valuable to the students when it is organized on democratic principles. The group should plan a constitution which states the purposes of the organization, policies of the group, duties of the officers, and procedures for functioning. The constitution should be planned to meet the

needs of the group in their own school, since the problems of administration and school functions vary with each school and thus require a particular organization.

The club should develop standards that are practical for the level of ability of the students in the group. It is not difficult to raise standards if one maintains a perspective in line with what it is possible to achieve. Selection of new members invariably becomes a problem when standards are raised. When the difference in skill between incoming students and the older members becomes too great, a policy of selection is necessary in order to maintain standards. Most dance clubs select new members by holding tryouts. The greatest problem in tryouts is knowing what to expect from those who try out, and whether or not what is expected is valid.

Probably the most valid over-all deciding factor in accepting or rejecting a student is the answer to the question, "Is the individual able to keep up creatively and technically with the established group so that both the individual and the group will benefit by her participation?" If the student is rejected, she should understand the reasons for such a decision and should be counselled on how to overcome her inadequacies through further training before trying out again. Most dance clubs require that students who try out take part in a lesson, improvise to any stimulus that is presented, and present a dance study which she herself has created. The student is often rated on items such as co-ordination, flexibility, rhythmic accuracy, spontaneity, and creative ability. The decision to accept or reject a student should be by majority vote of the dance club members. Discussion of students should be geared to ability and should not become involved in personal bickering.

All policies and decisions should be made by the club at large. This includes not only changes in the constitution, but other matters, such as participation in other productions, acceptance of dances for concerts, appropriation of funds for programs, and the sponsoring of outside productions. Following is a sample of a dance club constitution.

CONSTITUTION OF ....(name of club)....

ARTICLE I

Name

Section 1. The name of this organization shall be ...... (name) .... of .... (school) .... It shall be affiliated with the Athletic Association.

Purpose

Section 2. The purpose of this organization shall be first to offer to women and men students the opportunity for creative dance study, composition, and performance.

Section 3. Second, to stimulate interest in artistic and creative dance and to foster standards of performance, appreciation, and understanding of dance as an art form in the community.

Section 4. Third, to earn money to send one or more members of .... on a dance scholarship during vacation to a school chosen by the recipient. The recipient shall be chosen by a vote of the members, officers of the organization, faculty adviser, and Dean's office.

ARTICLE II

Membership

Section 1. Undergraduate, faculty, and alumni desiring membership shall pass tryouts.

Section 2. Tryouts are to be held twice a year—in fall and spring. A formerly active member of the group who becomes inactive for one semester or more must try out again if he wishes to be reinstated as an active member.

Section 3. New members shall be formally initiated into the group within a week after tryouts.

Section 4. Active membership is maintained by regular attendance and by participation in the activities of the organization.

Section 5. After two unexcused absences from regular meetings per semester, a member shall be so notified of her absence. After the third unexcused absence, that member is automatically dropped from the organization. Application for excused absences may be presented to the officers for approval.

Section 6. Honorary membership in the organization may be extended by invitation of the members. All the privileges of the organization are available to honorary members.

Section 7. . . . . shall have an associate membership consisting of persons interested in helping with activities correlated with productions.

ARTICLE III

Officers

Section 1. The officers of the organization shall be president, vice-president, secretary, and treasurer. These officers together with the faculty advisor of . . . . shall make up the board.

President

Section 2. It shall be the duty of the president to see that the constitution is carried out and to preside at all meetings.

Vice-President

Section 3. The vice-president shall carry out the duties of the president when the president is absent and will act as publicity director. He shall be in charge of writing and sending publicity to the school paper, local papers, *Dance Observer,* dance section of the *Journal of the AAHPER,*

and other such periodicals. He shall also clip
all newspaper and magazine publicity of the
organization and mount it in the . . . .
scrapbook. He shall choose his own committee.

Secretary

Section 4. It shall be the duty of the secretary to keep a
record of all proceedings and attendance. He
shall add correspondence to the . . . .
files and carry out Article II, Section 5. He
shall also keep an accurate list of the names and
local addresses of the members of . . . .
He shall conduct all correspondence of the organization.

Treasurer

Section 5. It shall be the duty of the treasurer to pay bills
and collect assessments. He shall file an annual
financial report in the offices of the Dean and
Comptroller. He shall file a financial report on
all concerts.

Costume and Stage Managers

Section 6. It shall be the duty of the costume manager to
be in charge of the care of costumes and costume rooms. Costumes shall not be loaned to
individuals or groups without the consent of
the . . . . officers. Costumes shall be
numbered and an accurate file kept on all incoming and outgoing costumes.

Section 7. The stage managers shall be responsible for
technical aspects of the performances. They
shall keep a record of all stage props owned
by . . . .

ARTICLE IV

Elections

Section 1. Candidates for office must have been a member
of . . . . for at least one semester.

Section 2. Officers shall hold office for one year only, but may be re-elected.

Section 3. Election of officers shall take place during a meeting in the spring. The . . . . board shall present a slate of officers at the meeting prior to elections. On the night of elections, nominations from the floor shall be accepted. Voting shall be by secret ballot.

ARTICLE V

Meetings

Section 1. There shall be one weekly meeting of the organization.

Section 2. Members stay for the entire meeting unless pre-excused. Tardiness shall be explained to members of the board. Meetings run from 7:15 P.M. to 9:30 P.M.

ARTICLE VI

Revision of the Constitution

Section 1. The constitution shall be amended by the proposal of any member and a three-fourths vote of all . . . . members. This proposal should be first presented to . . . . officers for discussion and then brought to the group.

ARTICLE VII

Concerts

Section 1. Absences from concert rehearsals must be excused in advance by the person in charge of the particular dance that will be missed. No excuses will be accepted from the concert rehearsals except for illness, required college functions, or emergency.

Recommendations

    1. Chairman of any special events shall hand in a detailed
       report of the committee's work not later than two weeks
       after the event.

    2. It is required that all . . . . members participate
       in a dance class.

METHODS OF FUNCTIONING

The group as a whole should discuss their plans for the year.
This includes the planning of any productions or participation
in productions of other organizations. During these discussions
the students may suggest ideas for dances or general ideas for
an annual production. The club president or faculty adviser
may stimulate the group to experiment with ideas which would
be suitable and possible for the group to handle. Often, the
ideas may arise out of class lessons or as a result of the dance
club meetings. It is usually best for the group to experiment
and think about ideas for a few weeks and then present them
at a definite time. When ideas and suggestions are presented,
the group can discuss and develop them further, decide whether
or not they should be adopted, and plan for the number of people needed for each dance. With good leadership it is possible
to have two or three different groups working at the same time.

Once the ideas are accepted and the students are grouped to
their satisfaction, it is necessary to have a group leader. The
leader functions in the capacity of an integrator who pulls the
loose ends together, sets problems to be solved, and organizes
the method of attack. She must be sure to keep the group functioning smoothly and to step in if there is difficulty. She must
be ingenious enough to get everyone to contribute at one time
or another. She sets the stage for evaluation of the work of
her group and considers the opinion of group members. Her
group as a whole decides what goes into their dance. Her job
is one of human relationships more than choreographing a
dance. It is the group leader's responsibility to get co-ordinated
functioning of the group so that the results will be a product

of the best efforts of that group. This is no small job, and group leaders need a great deal of supervision and counselling.

This type of organization requires experience with creative working methods as well as some dance background. If the dance background of the group has been creative, they are eager to choreograph their own dances. If they haven't been exposed sufficiently to creative work, it is necessary to prepare them for doing their own choroeography. Students generally take more pride in performing their own dances than those choreographed by someone else.

The different groups working on dances meet periodically to show to the rest of the club members what they have accomplished. They all take part in the evaluation of what they see. Once they begin to analyze the works of others, their own ideas begin to be tested. Everyone benefits from sharing success and failure if she applies what she learns to her own work. Through constructive criticism of other group members, students feel a stronger identification with their group, because they are contributing something that helps them come closer to accomplishing their goals.

The group must decide on a deadline for finishing dances that are to be given in a production. Dances should be completely finished, except for the polishing of fine points, at least two weeks before the performance date. This is necessary if the dances are to take any solid form. Two weeks is not ideal, but it is the most practical amount of time in light of other school pressures. There is also the problem of maintaining interest and a pitch of physical tension needed to give a good performance. These cannot be prolonged much beyond two weeks.

PERFORMANCE

Performance can be a very valuable experience if it is guided properly. Students who take part in dance productions should not be self-centered, either in their composition or performance. If the group adviser does a good job of guiding the development of the dances and gives criticism that will cause the student to redirect her efforts, the finished product should not be a personally involved one. If one inherits a self-centered individual in the group who is there because she loves to be in the limelight, it is necessary to devise some means of redirecting her energy and interests. If a student in the group does not develop in the desired direction, the adviser has slipped and needs to do an evaluation job on herself.

Dance is a performing art—it lives at its highest only during performance. To study and create dances and never perform them is to have an incomplete dance experience. The process of preparing a dance program, with all its related problems, can be a most worthwhile educational venture. Besides the extensive work involved in creating one's dances, the student must do a critical job of refining and reconstructing her ideas. She must constantly evaluate what she has done, in order to be sure that the results will be representative of finished and artistic student work. Such refinement puts her to a test of critical thinking and frustration tolerance out of which worthwhile results usually emerge.

To do a good job of performance, the student must learn to do her best within the limits of her ability; she must identify herself with a larger group, know her place in the group, and maintain it gracefully; she must learn to work closely with others during periods of intensive practice when fatigue sets off irritability; she must learn to be responsible for herself and the part she plays in running a smooth and effective performance.

In return for the months of work and preparation for performance, she receives the satisfaction of knowing that she has grown and accomplished what she set out to do. Before the production is over, she has ideas for new dances, she knows how differently she would attack another problem, and she is ready to explore further.

Beyond these very important results, the performance experience offers the student enjoyment and recognition by friends and associates whose opinions she values; and there are dozens of little exchanges and fleeting experiences which touch her deeply. These she carries in her own private storehouse of inspiring experiences and they are reflected in her attitude toward herself and others.

8

Summary

THE particular teaching method presented in this book is based on democratic principles. Education in general aims to establish principles of democratic living in each new generation. This book represents one method of achieving this aim. The student's role in education is one of satisfying her immediate needs and searching for a larger purpose in life. The teacher's role is one of providing the learning situation for the student and guiding the individual in her search. The teacher must be creative and ingenious in guiding the student's search constructively. Such educational methods foster the emergence of individuals who are a totality, who are capable of achieving well-adjusted lives in relation to their environment, who understand and accept principles of individual differences. Through such education an individual should develop a sense of values which will guide her in coping with problems of living.

The creative approach to dance provides one solution to the problem of educating for democratic living. This approach is based on the principle of guiding individual development through problem solving. The individual attack on such problems, as well as the solutions, may be varied. However, all solutions have certain common denominators. The problem-solving process takes the student on a journey of unexplored experiences in which she steers the course of development, makes the decisions, kindles her own motivation, and evaluates the success or failure of the venture. Such a venture enables the student to see many possible solutions to a problem. These experiences develop many paths of thinking, and they also develop the habits of thinking in relative rather than in absolute terms. Through such activity the student learns that no one has all the answers and that solutions to problems can evolve from many kinds of activity.

This book is an attempt to put into action, through the study of creative dance, the above-stated principles. The method used in achieving this aim is one which involves the student in a process which starts with the objective, becomes subjective, and culminates in a creative process which is then evaluated. In terms of a specific lesson, the teacher begins the lesson with a defined movement or sequence of movements which are based upon functional principles of body structure. Through guided experimentation with these movements or sequences, the student discovers, kinesthetically and emotionally, particular feeling states and associations within this experience. This is the stage of development when a student relates the movement experience to herself and it is referred to as "the subjective stage of experience." The student is then presented with a related problem to solve. In the solving of this problem she is experiencing the creative process. This, in essence, comprises the over-all approach to teaching dance creatively.

In Chapter 3, "Fundamental Movement Experiences," this plan is present. It is applied to the discovery of the most important muscle groups of the body. The physical progression in that chapter is based on the natural plan of physical development and maturation in human beings. In this plan, strength, co-ordination, and knowledge in using and controlling the large muscle groups of the body are of first consideration, with the development of small muscle groups following. Likewise, the progression of central control of the body necessarily comes before peripheral control. These fundamental movement experiences provide an opportunity for discovery of structural principles of bodily movement; they create an understanding of the possibilities and limitations of bodily movement; and they provide the beginning of the creative process through the presentation of small problems and the initiation into improvisation.

Gradual development of creative activity through fundamental movement experience prepares the student for more intensive work in improvisation and composition. When a student is thoroughly grounded in the kind of work outlined in Chapter 3, she is ready to pursue the study of improvisation and composition more thoroughly. Improvisation and composition are grouped together because they are an integral part of each other. Improvisation provides a free and broad background of movement experience to draw from when composing a dance. It is a resource for composition. On the other hand, the process of composing imposes a discipline on the student which requires her to reproduce and set the form of movements discovered during an improvisation. It requires the student to evaluate her improvisation and select from it the most appropriate movements expressing an idea. Improvisation is one means of finding movement for a composition by means of "sense" and "feel." Composition is a means of expressing what one has to say.

When a class has progressed to the point of studying composition intensively, the split between technique and composition occurs. This is due to the fact that composition is very time-consuming—it is impossible to do anything else within the same class hour. By this time the student should be grounded enough in fundamentals to be able to study technique and composition separately and relate them for herself. The ideal arrangement is to have a double hour to include both technique and composition in one class, but this is uncommon in most schools. However, at this point, technique should be clarified.

Technique is more than simply the physical execution of a

dance. It is the total process of expressing oneself, in which process the efficiency of execution is a very important part. In large measure, technique is self-discipline in adhering to the principles of movement stated in Chapter 3. Technique is popularly considered the perfection of physical execution of movements that train a dancer's body. But technique is much more inclusive than that. There are many phases of technique which cannot be developed through routine exercises. There are countless subtle nuances involved in movement expression which are an integral part of technique. The fine differentiation in movement which carries meaning cannot be developed solely through exercises, for such differentiations are dependent on motivation and understanding of relationship of movement to expression. This suggests that creative development is also a part of technique.

Too often the emphasis is placed on physical control by means of co-ordination and strengthening exercises. These exercises carry little expressive value in themselves. It is possible to motivate such exercises, but the motivation must come from the student. The student who does a good job of motivating her movement is one who has had the benefit of creative work. Teachers often expect the spontaneity and creative phase of a student's development to come about automatically. The results are much better if one teaches for such effects and guides the development of students in the direction of the more complete training. This necessitates ingenuity and planning on the part of the teacher.

Unfortunately, technique has come to be popularly thought of as training exercises for strength, flexibility, co-ordination, and rhythm; and then, on the other side of the fence, composition. This separation is not only arbitrary but impractical in an educational institution. It is impossible to separate the creative experience from its execution or execution from composition and have anything that resembles a dance. To say one is more important than the other is to admit they are not part of the same thing. It is understandable that during the learning process there are times when the emphasis must lean temporarily in one direction or another. Many students improve technically through creative work and improve creatively through emphasis on technical problems that were preventing them from adequately expressing their ideas.

The idea that choreography has a craft phase as well as an art phase is generally accepted; but to say one should know the craft thoroughly before handling the art is educationally unsound. It would be equally unsound to say one could achieve creative artistry without the craft. They are both important, but they are important only in terms of their value as coordinated tools for the total education of the individual.

Glossary

Abstraction: The process of varying movement from its natural form but retaining the essence of the natural form.

Ambiguous: Stimuli which are open to various interpretations; double meaning; lacking in clearness and definiteness.

Antiphonal: A dance form which calls for alternate response; i.e., question and answer or statement and rebuttal.

Art Form: The result of artistic selection of re-experienced emotional values which are fashioned into a form for expressive purposes.

Associations: Connection of ideas in thought, or an idea connected with or suggested by a subject or thought.

Canon: Identical repetition of a movement phrase by two voices, one of which starts the first phrase as the first voice finishes that phrase.

Choreographer: A person who creates dance composition.

Choreography: The art and craft of composing a dance; the construction and ordering of movement, phrasing, rhythm, design, dynamics.

Composition: Organization and grouping of different aspects of a work of art so as to achieve a unified whole.

Contemporary Dance: Dance which reflects the times in which it is produced (synonymous with modern dance).

Contraction: Change in muscle or muscle groups by which they become thickened and shortened.

Creative: Having the ability to create; quality of originality and productiveness.

Creative Group Project: A project which is the result of creative effort on the part of all members of a group.

Creative Process: A developmental process through which an individual discovers movement which expresses feeling.

Direction: The line of action produced as a result of movement.

Dynamics: The interplay of forces in movements of contrast, movements of motion and rest, psychological and emotional thematic contrast, and in rhythmic interplay. Such contrast may be simultaneous or alternating.

Emotional Line: The rise and fall of emotional tension characteristic of a particular experience. The emotional line of such an experience provides the motivation for the overall dynamic structure of the dance.

Explosive Movement: Movement which has a dynamic and percussive quality, i.e., a fast release of energy in a short time; movement which changes quickly from small to large, fast to slow, or from action to rest.

Extension: The act of stretching or lengthening to the fullest extent.

Experience: Knowledge or practical wisdom one has gained from what he has observed, encountered, or undergone.

Feeling States: Pleasant or painful sensations one experiences when moved emotionally. Emotional perception revealed by an artist in his work.

Focus: Concentration of one's thoughts, attention, and movement toward a central point of attraction or activity.

Form: Shape or appearance; configuration. Something that gives or determines shape; manner or style of arranging and co-ordinating parts for effective results. Form is developed in relation to the content of a dance. The content is the motivating factor which gives the dance form. (See *Composition,* page 150.)

Organic form: Movement based on the rise and fall of emotional states as they exist in the reliving of the experience on which the dance is based.

Rhythmic form: The tempo, phrasing, meter, and rhythmic organization in general which binds movement into an organized whole. The essential rhythm is a result of organic movement.

Spatial Form: The relationship of the dancer and his movement to spatial forces.

Fundamental Movement Experience: Those movement experiences which serve as a foundation or basis on which one may develop technically and creatively. The motor aspect is based on the structure of the body and the laws governing motion. The psychological aspect is based on the principle of individual discovery and association of ideas with movement.

Gesture: A movement symbol which carries a specific meaning. It may be a movement of the head, body, arms, hands, or face. It expresses an idea, attitude, or emotional state.

Ground Base: A form of composition in which a short, fundamental part of the theme is continuously repeated throughout the whole composition. It may be done by several people or groups at different times but is always present somewhere in the composition.

Improvise: To compose extemporaneously or on the spur of the moment.

Inhibition: The blocking of one psychological process by another psychological process. One's inability to discipline his thoughts to free himself for expression.

Insight: The sudden grasping of a solution to a problem. The ability to see into inner character or underlying truth.

Intellectualized Composition: Composing a dance by planning movement intellectually as a carrier of meaning, as opposed to the organic approach.

Kinesthetic Perception: The muscular sensation which one feels as a result of movement. The sensations are the result of stimulation of proprioceptors or nerve endings in the muscles, tendons, and joints through pressure from muscle action. The impulses carried to the higher centers of the brain give the individual information about the force, range, and direction of movement.

Level: The various degrees of height from the floor upward, i.e., lying, sitting, kneeling, squatting, standing, jumping.

Locomotor: Movement which travels through space from one place to another.

Lunge: A thrust, plunge, or any sudden forward movement.

Metrical Rhythm: Rhythm which is regular and marked metrically as contrasted to breath rhythm which is based on the timing of movement in its natural and not necessarily metric form.

Mirroring Movement: A device for reproducing movement of another person simultaneously while the movement is being performed.

Mood: Frame of mind or state of feeling at a particular time.

Motor Imagery: Reliving of the sensations of an experience in the absence of the original stimulus. Formation of images as a result of experiences remembered or created through the imagination.

Movement Design: Creation of movement into an organized plan which is visually sculptural and striking. Movement which is designed to give a particular feeling.

Movement Dimension: The size or magnitude of movement from the body center toward one or more of three principal directional poles; horizontal, vertical, and depth.

Movement Through a Curved Path: Movement which is continuous and moves through space in a curved direction.

Natural Rhythm: The rhythmic organization in which a movement exists when it is created.

Objective: Belonging to the object of thought rather than to the thinking subject. A phase in the creative process in which the individual's thinking is taking a direction away from himself and his efforts are directed toward the subject matter and the form of expression it should take for communication.

Organic Dance: Dance which grows out of the emotional structure of an experience. The outward, observable form of the movement communicates the emotional impact because it is closely related to the emotional response people have experienced in situations similar to that being expressed.

Pantomime: Movement which describes the actions of a person in a particular situation.

Percussive Movement: Movement with a great deal of sudden force as in striking, exploding; movement which is quick, sharp, and staccato.

Perspective: A mental view of the relationship of parts to one another and to the whole.

Phrase: A sequence of movements which are so related as to give a sense of unity and organization.

Projection: The contact the dancer makes with an audience. A concentration on directing one's movement to an audience. Delivery, giving out to an audience.

Prop: Furniture, stage sets, ornament, and decorative objects used by the dancer to enhance communication.

Pulse: The underlying beat of rhythmic vibrations. A recurring rhythm or undulation whose regularity is a result of physical motivation from within.

Quality: Character or nature of movement which distinguishes it from other movement.

Range: Pertaining to size of movement; the extent or limits between which variation is possible.

Realistic: Movement in its natural form such as pantomime or gesture; movement as we know it in its practical existence.

Realization: Making real something that was imagined or planned; a principle becoming real when discovered through practical experience.

Resultant Rhythm: The rhythm which results from primary accents of two different meters.

Rhythm Structure: (see *Form*).

Round: A short rhythmical canon in which several voices may enter at equal intervals of time. Each voice is represented by a varying movement sequence.

Sequence: Continuous series of movements; succession of movements following one after another.

Space: (see *Form*).

Spatial Relationships: The atmosphere which is the result of the organization of movement to produce feeling of contracting, expanding, or limited space. This atmosphere may also include texture of space in addition to the individual or group orientation in space.

Spontaneity: Proceeding from a natural, personal impulse without effort or premeditation; natural and unrestrained impulses, movements, and actions.

Stimulus: Something that incites feeling states and thoughts to action.

Subjective: Existing in the intellect; belonging to the thinking subject rather than to the object of thought.

Suspension: The highest point in the rise of a movement just preceding its falling phase; the highest point in elevation preceding its descent. This phase of movement is lengthened, giving a quality of floating and lightness or detachment from gravity.

Suspension Point: The part of the body through which one feels the greatest vertical pull; resistance to gravity making one feel light and lifted.

Sustained Movement: Movement in which the action is carried on for a long period of time; movement in which the release of energy is steady and continuous.

Swing: A quality of pendular movement characterized by an initial force, momentum, and suspension.

Symbolism: A vehicle of communication through representation.

Technique: Skill in over-all performance.

Tempo: Relative rate of speed of movement.

Tensional Relationships: An oppositional relationship of parts of the body to each other or of movements of one person to another which create a tensional pull in opposing directions.

Torso: The trunk of the human body.

Traction: The attractive force between the body and a point around which it travels; an adhesive quality which is found particularly in locomotor movement through a curved path.

Undulation: Movement which has the quality of a wave; an alternate rise and fall.

Unison: Two or more people performing the same movement at the same time.

Variation: Transformation of a theme; deviation of movement from a set theme or norm; change in condition, character, or degree.

Vibration: Movement that oscillates or has a tremulous quality; produced by alternate contractions of opposing muscle groups at a rapid rate of speed and resulting in an extreme degree of muscular tension.

INDEX

Index